HIGH TRIGLYCERIDES DIET COOKBOOK

2100 Days of Nutritious Recipes for Heart-Health and Lowering High Triglycerides (28 days meal plan)

By

Grantle Pendliy

TABLE OF CONTENTS

INTRODUCTION 7

CHAPTER 1: WHAT ARE HIGH TRIGLYCERIDES, CAUSES, AND SYMPTOMS? 8

    IT'S SYMPTOMS 8
    DIAGNOSTIC OF HIGH TRIGLYCERIDES 9
    THE DANGERS OF HIGH TRIGLYCERIDES 10

CHAPTER 2: HOW TO REDUCE TRIGLYCERIDES 12

    WHO IS IN DANGER? 12
    WHEN YOU HAVE HIGH TRIGLYCERIDES AND HEALTHY HABITS AREN'T ENOUGH TO HELP YOU .. 13
    DETECTING HIGH TRIGLYCERIDES 13
    HOW TO REDUCE TRIGLYCERIDE LEVELS 14

CHAPTER 3: FOOD TO AVOID AND FOOD TO EAT 16

    FOOD TO EAT HEALTHY 16
    FOOD TO AVOID 17

CHAPTER 4: RECIPES FOR BREAKFAST 18

    GREEK YOGURT PARFAIT: 18
    EGG AND VEGETABLE SCRAMBLE: 19
    WHOLE GRAIN OATMEAL WITH BERRIES AND ALMONDS: 20
    AVOCADO TOAST WITH TOMATOES AND SPROUTS: 21
    SWEET POTATO HASH WITH EGGS: 22
    GREEK YOGURT WITH FRUIT AND NUTS: 22
    BREAKFAST QUINOA BOWL WITH BERRIES AND NUTS: 23
    SMOKED SALMON AND SCRAMBLED EGGS: 23
    HOMEMADE GRANOLA WITH YOGURT AND BERRIES: 24
    SPINACH AND FETA OMELETTE: 25
    COTTAGE CHEESE WITH PINEAPPLE AND WALNUTS: 26
    CHIA SEED PUDDING WITH BERRIES: 26
    VEGGIE BREAKFAST BURRITO WITH BLACK BEANS AND SALSA: 27
    TUNA SALAD ON WHOLE GRAIN TOAST: 27
    BAKED SWEET POTATO WITH GREEK YOGURT AND BERRIES: 28
    TURKEY AND EGG BREAKFAST SANDWICH ON WHOLE GRAIN ENGLISH MUFFIN: 29
    OVERNIGHT OATS WITH ALMOND BUTTER AND BANANA: 30
    BAKED EGG AND VEGGIE CUPS: 30

Apple Cinnamon Quinoa Porridge: 31
Chickpea and Vegetable Scramble: 32
Zucchini Fritters with Poached Eggs: 33
Smoked Salmon Bagel with Cream Cheese and Cucumber: 34
Mushroom and Spinach Frittata: 34
Egg White and Vegetable Wrap: 35
Berry Smoothie with Chia Seeds and Almond Milk: 36
Chocolate Banana Protein Pancakes: 37
Shakshuka with Feta Cheese and Whole Grain Bread: 38
Egg and Avocado Salad on Whole Grain Toast: 39
Blueberry Protein Waffles: 40
Cauliflower Rice and Egg Breakfast Bowl: 41

CHAPTER 5: RECIPES FOR LUNCH 42

Grilled Chicken Salad with Mixed Greens and Veggies: 42
Broiled Salmon with Roasted Vegetables: 43
Tuna Salad with Leafy Greens and Cherry Tomatoes: 44
Turkey and Avocado Wrap with Whole Wheat Tortilla: 45
Lentil Soup with Carrots and Celery: 46
Grilled Shrimp Skewers with Quinoa Salad: 47
Grilled Tofu and Vegetable Kebabs: 48
Mixed Vegetable Stir-Fry with Brown Rice: 49
Chicken and Vegetable Soup: 50
Baked Salmon with Asparagus and Sweet Potato: 51
Chickpea Salad with Cucumbers and Tomatoes: 51
Turkey and Vegetable Chili: 52
Grilled Chicken and Vegetable Kabobs: 53
Broiled Fish with Steamed Vegetables: 54
Black Bean and Vegetable Enchiladas: 55
Turkey Burger with Whole Wheat Bun and Side Salad: 56
Shrimp and Vegetable Stir-Fry with Brown Rice: 57
Lentil and Vegetable Curry: 58
Grilled Portobello Mushroom and Veggie Wrap: 60
Baked Chicken with Green Beans and Carrots: 61
Tofu and Vegetable Stir-Fry with Brown Rice: 62
Spinach and Feta Stuffed Chicken Breast: 63
Roasted Vegetable and Chickpea Bowl: 64
Grilled Shrimp with Brown Rice and Vegetables: 65

Turkey and Vegetable Skewers with Quinoa Salad: 66
Vegetable and Tofu Curry: 67
Broiled Fish with Vegetable Skewers: 68
Baked Chicken with Roasted Vegetables: 69
Quinoa and Vegetable Stuffed Bell Peppers: 69
Lentil and Vegetable Soup with Whole Grain Bread: 70

CHAPTER 6: RECIPES FOR DINNER 72

Grilled Chicken with Roasted Vegetables: 72
Broiled Salmon with Quinoa and Spinach Salad: 73
Turkey Meatballs with Zucchini Noodles: 74
Baked Cod with Lemon and Herbs: 75
Lentil and Vegetable Stew with Brown Rice: 76
Grilled Tofu and Vegetable Kebabs with Brown Rice: 77
Pan-Seared Scallops with Asparagus and Quinoa: 78
Stuffed Bell Peppers with Ground Turkey and Quinoa: 79
Chickpea and Vegetable Curry with Whole Wheat Naan 80
Spaghetti Squash with Turkey Bolognese Sauce: 81
Grilled Shrimp Skewers with Avocado and Tomato Salad: 82
Baked Chicken with Green Beans and Tomatoes: 83
Seared Tuna with Sesame Ginger Sauce and Broccoli: 84
Vegetable and Tofu Stir-Fry with Brown Rice: 85
Grilled Steak with Roasted Brussels Sprouts and Sweet Potato Wedges 86
Quinoa Stuffed Acorn Squash with Cranberries and Walnuts: 87
Broiled Flounder with Ratatouille: 88
Lentil and Vegetable Shepherd's Pie with Sweet Potato Topping: 89
Baked Eggplant Parmesan with Whole Grain Pasta: 90
Vegetable Fajitas with Guacamole and Salsa: 92
Chicken and Vegetable Skewers with Cauliflower Rice: 93
Grilled Pork Tenderloin with Grilled Vegetables and Brown Rice: 94
Quinoa Stuffed Peppers with Black Beans and Corn: 95
Zucchini Noodles with Shrimp and Tomato Sauce: 96
Grilled Vegetable and Goat Cheese Quesadillas: 97
Baked Salmon with Broccoli and Cauliflower Gratin: 98
Chicken and Vegetable Stir-Fry with Brown Rice: 99
Lentil and Vegetable Tacos with Whole Wheat Tortillas: 100
Shrimp and Vegetable Curry with Brown Rice: 101
Baked Cod with Roasted Red Pepper Sauce and Sautéed Spinach: 103

CHAPTER 7: RECIPES FOR DESSERT 104

Fresh fruit salad with Greek yogurt and honey: 104
Baked apples with cinnamon and walnuts: 105
Chocolate avocado pudding: 106
Berry and yogurt parfait with granola: 107
Poached pears with honey and cinnamon: 108
Grilled pineapple with Greek yogurt and honey: 109
Mixed berry crumble with almond flour topping: 110
Chia seed pudding with coconut milk and mango: 111
Peach and blueberry crisp with oatmeal topping: 112
Lemon poppy seed muffins with almond flour: 113
Dark chocolate and almond butter bites: 114
Mixed berry smoothie with almond milk and chia seeds: 115
Blueberry and Greek yogurt popsicles: 115
Apple cinnamon oatmeal cookies with coconut flour: 116
Strawberry and avocado smoothie bowl: 117
Chocolate and peanut butter protein balls: 118
Mango and coconut chia seed pudding: 118
Roasted pears with balsamic glaze and walnuts: 119
Vegan banana bread with almond flour and coconut oil: 120
Orange and almond flour cake with honey glaze: 121
Coconut and almond flour cookies with dark chocolate chips: 122
Chocolate and cherry chia seed pudding: 123
Peanut butter and a jelly smoothie with almond milk and chia seeds: 123
Carrot and walnut muffins with coconut flour: 124
Greek yogurt and berry ice cream with honey: 125
Vanilla and almond flour cupcakes with Greek yogurt frosting: 126
Grilled peaches with honey and cinnamon: 127
Apple and almond butter crumble with oatmeal topping: 128
Chocolate and raspberry smoothie bowl: 129
Coconut and almond flour pancakes with fresh berries: 130

CHAPTER 8: RECIPES FOR SMACKS 131

Apple slices with almond butter: 131
Carrot sticks with hummus: 132
Hard-boiled eggs: 132
Apple slices with almond butter: *Ingredients:* 133
Carrot sticks with hummus: 133

Hard-boiled eggs:	133
Greek yogurt with mixed berries:	134
Sliced cucumber with tzatziki sauce:	134
Trail mix with nuts and dried fruit:	134
Edamame:	135
Roasted chickpeas:	135
Dark chocolate squares:	136
Cherry tomatoes with feta cheese:	137
Cottage cheese with pineapple chunks:	137
Avocado and tomato salsa with whole grain chips:	138
Popcorn with nutritional yeast:	138
Turkey and cheese roll-ups:	139
Energy balls with nuts and dried fruit:	139
Baked sweet potato fries:	140
Grilled zucchini with Parmesan cheese:	140
Ants on a log (celery with peanut butter and raisins):	142
Roasted almonds with sea salt:	142
Tuna salad with whole grain crackers:	143
Homemade kale chips:	143
Sliced bell pepper with guacamole:	144
Apple slices with cinnamon and honey:	144
Smoked salmon with cucumber slices:	145
Banana and almond butter bites:	145
Greek yogurt with honey and granola:	145
Quinoa salad with vegetables:	146
Baked kale chips with garlic and Parmesan:	147
Watermelon cubes with feta cheese:	147
Hummus and vegetable wraps:	148

CHAPTER 9: 28-DAYS MEAL PLAN 149

First week	149
Second week	151
Third week	153
Fourth week	155

CONCLUSION 157

INTRODUCTION

Triglycerides are fat found in the blood that is vital to energy metabolism. However, when levels of triglycerides become too high, it can increase the risk of developing heart disease, stroke, and other health problems.

Fortunately, diet plays a crucial role in managing triglyceride levels. A high triglycerides diet focuses on reducing the intake of foods that can increase triglyceride levels, such as saturated and trans fats, and increasing the intake of foods that can lower triglycerides, such as fiber and omega-3 fatty acids.

In addition to dietary changes, other lifestyle modifications, such as regular exercise and weight management, can also help to lower triglyceride levels.

Working with a healthcare provider or registered dietitian is essential to determine the best dietary approach for managing triglyceride levels based on individual health needs and medical history. With a balanced and heart-healthy diet, it's possible to lower triglyceride levels and reduce the risk of developing related health problems.

CHAPTER 1: WHAT ARE HIGH TRIGLYCERIDES, CAUSES, AND SYMPTOMS?

Triglyceride levels that are abnormally high in the blood are high triglycerides. The body uses triglycerides, fat that circulates in the bloodstream, as energy. Triglyceride levels, however, can raise the risk of heart disease, stroke, and other health issues if they become too high.

Adults typically have triglyceride blood levels of less than 150 milligrams per deciliter (mg/dL). While very high levels are 500 mg/dL or more, borderline-high levels are between 150 and 199 mg/dL, 200 to 499 mg/dL, and 300 to 499 mg/dL.

Obesity, insulin resistance, and metabolic syndrome are other disorders frequently linked to high triglyceride levels. Specific drugs and medical conditions can also cause elevated triglyceride levels. In some situations, a healthy diet, regular exercise, and weight loss may be advised in addition to medicine to lower high triglyceride levels.

IT'S SYMPTOMS

Most of those with high triglyceride levels don't exhibit any particular symptoms. Frequently, the illness is discovered through routine blood tests that evaluate triglyceride and cholesterol levels. High triglyceride levels, however, might occasionally result in symptoms like:

*1. **Pancreatitis:** In a small percentage of instances, extremely high triglyceride levels (over 1000 mg/dL) can result in pancreatic inflammation, which can be life-threatening. Pancreatitis* symptoms include excruciating stomach pain, nausea, vomiting, and fever.

2. Skin changes: Excessive triglyceride levels can result in xanthomas, fatty deposits under the skin. These deposits can develop on the hands, feet, elbows, or buttocks and often take the form of tiny, yellowish pimples.

3. Abnormal blood lipid profile: High triglycerides are frequently accompanied by additional lipid abnormalities, such as high total cholesterol, low HDL, and high LDL cholesterol. The risk of heart disease can rise as a result of certain anomalies.

It's crucial to remember that most people with high triglyceride levels have no symptoms. Therefore, routine blood testing is essential to identify elevated triglyceride levels and other lipid disorders.

DIAGNOSTIC OF HIGH TRIGLYCERIDES

With the help of a quick blood test known as a lipid profile, high triglycerides can be identified. To obtain an accurate readout of the lipid levels in the bloodstream, this test is often performed after a 9-12 hour fast. A lipid profile test analyzes several different triglyceride and cholesterol levels in the blood, such as:

1. **Total cholesterol:** The combined amount of "good" and "bad" cholesterol in the bloodstream.
2. Low-density lipoprotein (LDL) cholesterol, also called "bad" cholesterol, can accumulate in artery walls and raise the risk of heart disease. High-density lipoprotein (HDL) cholesterol: Known as the "good" cholesterol, HDL cholesterol helps remove LDL cholesterol from the bloodstream.

1. **Triglycerides**: A type of fat that circulates in the bloodstream and can contribute to heart disease risk.

The American Heart Association recommends that adults have a lipid profile test every four to six years as part of routine health care. If a person has risk factors for heart disease, such as a family history of heart disease, diabetes, or high blood pressure, more frequent testing may be recommended. If high triglyceride levels are detected, lifestyle changes, medication, or other interventions may be recommended to lower them and reduce the risk of heart disease.

THE DANGERS OF HIGH TRIGLYCERIDES

High triglycerides can increase the risk of developing several health complications, including:

1. **Cardiovascular disease:** Heart disease and stroke risk are both elevated by high triglyceride levels. Increased triglycerides can contribute to the development of fatty arterial deposits that cause atherosclerosis, a condition in which the arteries constrict and harden.
2. Pancreatitis: Inflammation of the pancreas can result from extremely high triglyceride levels (over 1000 mg/dL), which can be a medical emergency. The symptoms of pancreatitis include fever, nausea, vomiting, and severe stomach pain.
3. **Metabolic syndrome:** This group of disorders includes high blood pressure, high blood sugar, and excess body fat around the waist. One of its components is excessive triglyceride levels. The metabolic syndrome increases the risk of type 2 diabetes, heart disease, and stroke.

4. **Nonalcoholic fatty liver disease:** Elevated triglycerides may be a factor in the development of nonalcoholic fatty liver disease, characterized by fat accumulation in the liver. Nonalcoholic fatty liver disease over time might result in liver injury and potentially liver failure.
5. **Type 2 diabetes:** High triglyceride levels can cause insulin resistance, in which the body's cells lose their receptivity to the hormone. Type 2 diabetes and elevated blood sugar levels can be caused by insulin resistance.

It's crucial to remember that many of these issues can be avoided or controlled by lifestyle changes, such as adopting a nutritious diet, engaging in regular exercise, losing weight, and taking medication in some circumstances. A healthcare professional can suggest the most effective strategies to lower high triglyceride levels and lessen the risk of these issues. They can also assist in determining the underlying reasons for these problems.

CHAPTER 2: HOW TO REDUCE TRIGLYCERIDES

Your blood contains a specific sort of fat called triglycerides. Your chance of developing heart disease and other health issues can increase if your triglyceride levels are high. The following advice will help you lower your triglyceride levels:

WHO IS IN DANGER?

People who have one or more of the following risk factors may be more likely to have high triglyceride levels:

1. Being overweight or obese
2. A diet that is unhealthy and incredibly heavy in sugar and processed carbohydrates
3. Lack of physical activity or exercise
4. Smoking
5. Abusing booze too much
6. Insulin resistance or diabetes
7. Thyroid problems
8. Kidney illness
9. Liver illness
10. High triglyceride levels run in the family or are inherited

If you have high triglycerides, you must monitor your levels frequently and take steps to lower your risk. Maintaining a healthy lifestyle will help lower triglycerides and lessen your risk of heart disease and other health issues. Examples of such a lifestyle include exercising frequently, eating a balanced diet, and avoiding excessive alcohol and sugary foods. If lifestyle changes alone are insufficient to lower triglyceride levels, your doctor may additionally suggest medicines.

WHEN YOU HAVE HIGH TRIGLYCERIDES AND HEALTHY HABITS AREN'T ENOUGH TO HELP YOU

Sometimes, altering one's lifestyle may not reduce excessive triglyceride levels. Your doctor could suggest drugs to help lower triglycerides if you've made healthy modifications to your diet and exercise regimen, but your stories have stayed the same. Among the typical medications used to treat high triglycerides are:

1. **Statins:** These drugs can also lower triglycerides and are often used to lower cholesterol.
2. **Fibrates:** Fibrates can increase HDL cholesterol (the "good" cholesterol) and lower triglycerides.
3. Supplements containing omega-3 fatty acids may reduce triglycerides.
4. **Niacin:** Niacin can increase HDL cholesterol and reduce triglycerides.

It is crucial to discuss the ideal course of treatment with your doctor. They can suggest the best course of action for treating your excessive triglycerides and assist in identifying the underlying reason.

DETECTING HIGH TRIGLYCERIDES

A quick blood test can identify high triglyceride levels. A blood test called a lipid panel or lipid profile measures different triglycerides and cholesterol levels in your blood. If you have other heart disease risk factors or your doctor suspects you have excessive triglycerides, they may request a lipid panel. The following measures are frequently included in the lipid panel:

1. Total cholesterol: This indicator shows the total quantity of LDL (the "bad" cholesterol) and HDL (the "good" cholesterol) in your blood.
2. LDL cholesterol gauges the quantity of LDL, or "bad" cholesterol, in your blood.
3. HDL cholesterol: This gauges the quantity of HDL cholesterol, or "good" cholesterol, in your blood.
4. Triglycerides: This gauges how many triglycerides are present in your blood.

To calculate your overall risk for heart disease, your doctor may also request further tests or assess other risk factors, such as your weight, blood pressure, and family history of heart disease. It's crucial to test and monitor your cholesterol and triglyceride levels according to your doctor's advice.

HOW TO REDUCE TRIGLYCERIDE LEVELS

You can lower your triglyceride levels by altering your lifestyle and eating well. Here are some recommendations for reducing triglycerides:

1. Eat a balanced diet of fruits, vegetables, whole grains, lean proteins, and healthy fats such as the omega-3 fatty acids in fish, nuts, and vegetable oils. 1. Eat a nutritious diet.
2. Reduce your intake of sugar and refined carbs: White bread, pasta, and other refined carbohydrates, as well as sugary foods and drinks, can raise your triglyceride levels.
3. Regular exercise is essential. Aim to do moderate-intensity exercise for at least 30 minutes per day.
4. Maintaining a healthy weight will help lower your triglycerides if you are overweight.

5. Drink in moderation: Excessive alcohol consumption might cause triglycerides to rise. Limit your alcohol consumption to no more than one drink for ladies and two for men daily.
6. Give up smoking: Smoking raises triglycerides and heart disease risk.
7. Take care of underlying health issues: Manage any underlying health issues that may be a factor in high triglyceride levels, such as diabetes or high blood pressure.
8. Take medication: Your doctor may advise statins, fibrates, or omega-3 fatty acids to assist in lowering your triglyceride levels if they continue to be high despite lifestyle adjustments.

Before beginning a new medicine or making any lifestyle changes, it is crucial to see your doctor. Based on your medical requirements, they can assist you in choosing the optimal treatment course.

CHAPTER 3: FOOD TO AVOID AND FOOD TO EAT

FOOD TO EAT HEALTHY

Eating a balanced diet is one of the most crucial measures for lowering triglyceride levels. Here are some food suggestions that may be useful:

1. Reduce your intake of saturated and trans fats because they can cause triglycerides to rise. Steer clear of processed snacks, fried foods, fatty meats, and other items high in these fats.
2. Emphasize healthy fats: Fish, nuts, and vegetable oils contain monounsaturated and polyunsaturated fats that can reduce triglycerides. Increase the amount of these beneficial fats in your diet.
3. Go for whole grains: Fiber-rich entire grains have the potential to reduce triglycerides. Pick whole-grain versions of bread, pasta, and cereal over refined ones.
4. Consume many fruits and vegetables: Fruits and vegetables are a healthy choice for reducing triglycerides because they are high in fiber and low in calories.
5. Consume less sugar and processed carbohydrates: White bread, pasta, and other refined carbohydrates, as well as sugary foods and drinks, can raise triglyceride levels. Limit the amount of these things you eat.
6. Include lean protein sources: Lean protein is good for decreasing triglycerides and can be found in foods including fish, poultry, and tofu.
7. Limit your alcohol intake: Drinking too much can increase triglycerides. Limit your alcohol consumption to no more than one drink for ladies and two for men daily.

Before making any significant dietary changes, remember to consult your doctor. They can assist you in developing a meal plan specifically for your health requirements.

FOOD TO AVOID

Avoiding or restricting certain foods is crucial for lowering your triglyceride levels. These foods should be avoided:

1. Sugar-rich foods and beverages: Foods and drinks with a lot of sugar might raise triglyceride levels. Avoid or consume in moderation sugary foods, sweets, and beverages.
2. Refined carbohydrates: White bread, pasta, and rice prepared with white flour can raise triglyceride levels. Instead, pick the whole-grain varieties of these meals.
3. Saturated and trans fats can cause triglycerides to increase. Foods high in saturated and trans fats, such as fatty meats, fried items, and processed snacks, should be avoided or limited.
4. Fried foods: Fried foods frequently contain many calories and bad fats, which can cause triglycerides to rise.
5. Alcohol: Excessive alcohol consumption can increase triglycerides. Limit your alcohol consumption to no more than one drink for ladies and two for men daily.
6. Dairy items with high-fat content, such as cheese and cream, might include a lot of saturated fat, which increases triglycerides. Instead, go for low- or no-fat varieties of these items.

Before making any significant dietary changes, remember to consult your doctor. They can assist you in developing a meal plan specifically for your health requirements.

CHAPTER 4: RECIPES FOR BREAKFAST

GREEK YOGURT PARFAIT:

Ingredients:

- 1 cup Greek yogurt
- 1/2 cup fresh berries (blueberries, raspberries, strawberries)
- 1/4 cup sliced almonds
- 1 tsp honey (optional)

Instructions:

1. Spoon half of the Greek yogurt into a bowl or glass.
2. Spread the yogurt with half of the fresh berries.
3. Add another layer of yogurt and berries after that.
4. Add sliced almonds on top.
5. If desired, drizzle honey over the top.

Optional: Adding a sprinkle of cinnamon or a drizzle of maple syrup on top adds flavor. Enjoy!

EGG AND VEGETABLE SCRAMBLE:

Ingredients:

- Two eggs
- 1/4 cup chopped onion
- 1/4 cup chopped bell pepper
- 1/4 cup chopped zucchini
- Salt and pepper to taste
- 1 tbsp olive oil

Instructions:

1. Beat the eggs with salt and pepper in a small bowl.
2. In a skillet over medium heat, warm the olive oil.
3. Include the diced onion, bell pepper, and zucchini. Sauté for 2–3 minutes or until the vegetables are just beginning to soften.
4. Pour the beaten eggs into the skillet and stir constantly when the eggs are cooked and scrambled.
5. Plate hot, and savor!

WHOLE GRAIN OATMEAL WITH BERRIES AND ALMONDS:

Ingredients:

- 1/2 cup rolled oats
- 1 cup water or milk
- 1/2 cup fresh berries (blueberries, raspberries, strawberries)
- 1/4 cup sliced almonds
- 1 tsp honey (optional)

Instructions:

1. Bring the oats and milk or water to a boil in a small pot.
2. Once the oats are cooked, and the mixture has thickened, lower the heat to a simmer and cook it for 5 to 7 minutes, stirring regularly.
3. Turn off the heat and allow to cool for a moment.
4. Add sliced almonds and fresh berries to the oatmeal for decoration.
5. If desired, drizzle honey on top and savor!

AVOCADO TOAST WITH TOMATOES AND SPROUTS:

Ingredients:

- One slice of whole grain bread toasted
- 1/2 ripe avocado, mashed
- 1/4 cup chopped cherry tomatoes
- 1/4 cup sprouts
- Salt and pepper to taste

Instructions:

1. Heat the milk or water and oats in a small pot until they are boiling.
2. Reduce the heat to a simmer and boil the mixture for 5 to 7 minutes, stirring often, once the oats have finished cooking and the mixture has thickened.
3. Please turn off the heat and give it a moment to cool.
4. Top the oats with sliced almonds and fresh berries as a finishing touch.
5. Drizzle honey over top if you like, then enjoy!

SWEET POTATO HASH WITH EGGS:

Ingredients:
- 1 large sweet potato, peeled and diced into small cubes
- 1 small onion, diced
- 1 red bell pepper, diced
- 2 tbsp olive oil
- Salt and pepper to taste
- 2 eggs

Instructions:
1. In a skillet over medium-high heat, warm the olive oil.
2. Add the cooked and slightly crispy sweet potato, onion, bell pepper, and sauté for 8 to 10 minutes, stirring regularly.
3. To taste, add salt and pepper to the dish.
4. Fry two eggs to your preferred doneness in a different skillet.
5. Plate the fried eggs on top of the sweet potato hash and serve.

GREEK YOGURT WITH FRUIT AND NUTS:

Ingredients:
- 1 cup Greek yogurt
- 1/2 cup mixed fresh fruit (such as blueberries, strawberries, and chopped peaches)
- 1/4 cup mixed nuts (such as almonds and walnuts)
- 1 tsp honey (optional)

Instructions:

1. Pour a bowl with the Greek yogurt.
2. Add a layer of mixed nuts and fresh fruit on top.
3. If desired, add honey on the top.
4. Dish out and savor!

BREAKFAST QUINOA BOWL WITH BERRIES AND NUTS:

Ingredients:
- 1 cup cooked quinoa
- 1/2 cup mixed fresh berries (such as blueberries, raspberries, and blackberries)
- 1/4 cup mixed nuts (such as almonds and pecans)
- 1 tbsp honey
- 1/4 cup milk (optional)

Instructions:
1. Combine the cooked quinoa, fresh berries, and nuts in a bowl.
2. Add honey to the mixture and whisk to blend.
3. If you want a creamier consistency, add milk.
4. Dish out and savor!

SMOKED SALMON AND SCRAMBLED EGGS:

Ingredients:
- 2 eggs
- 1 tbsp butter
- 2 oz smoked salmon, chopped
- Salt and pepper to taste
- 1 tbsp chopped chives

Instructions:

1. Beat the eggs with salt and pepper in a small bowl.
2. In a skillet over medium heat, melt the butter.
3. Add the beaten eggs and smoked salmon to the skillet and cook/scramble the eggs while stirring constantly.
4. Add chopped chives to the dish for taste.
5. Plate hot, and savor!

HOMEMADE GRANOLA WITH YOGURT AND BERRIES:

Ingredients:

- 2 cups rolled oats
- 1/2 cup sliced almonds
- 1/2 cup unsweetened shredded coconut
- 1/4 cup honey
- 1/4 cup coconut oil
- 1/2 tsp vanilla extract
- Pinch of salt
- 1 cup Greek yogurt
- 1/2 cup mixed fresh berries (such as blueberries, raspberries, and strawberries)

Instructions:

1. Set oven temperature to 350°F (175°C).
2. Combine the rolled oats, almond slices, and unsweetened coconut shreds in a mixing bowl.
3. Combine the honey, coconut oil, vanilla essence, and salt in another bowl.
4. After adding the honey mixture, whisk the oat mixture.

5. Place the mixture in a single layer on a baking sheet and bake for 20 to 25 minutes, stirring halfway through, or until crisp and golden brown.
6. Allow the granola to finish cooling.
7. Place the Greek yogurt in a bowl and top with the homemade granola and various fresh berries.
8. Dish out and savor!

SPINACH AND FETA OMELETTE:

Ingredients:
- 2 eggs
- 1/2 cup fresh spinach, chopped
- 1/4 cup crumbled feta cheese
- Salt and pepper to taste
- 1 tbsp butter

Instructions:
1. In a small bowl, beat the eggs with salt and pepper.
1. Beat the eggs with salt and pepper in a small bowl.
2. In a skillet over medium heat, melt the butter.
3. Stir in the beaten eggs and spinach, then simmer the mixture in the skillet for a few minutes.
4. When the eggs begin to set, top half the omelet with the crumbled feta cheese.
5. Carefully fold the other side of the omelet over the cheese using a spatula.
6. Allow to simmer for another minute or until the eggs are done to your preference and the cheese has melted.
7. Plate hot, and savor!

COTTAGE CHEESE WITH PINEAPPLE AND WALNUTS:

Ingredients:
- 1/2 cup low-fat cottage cheese
- 1/2 cup fresh pineapple chunks
- 1/4 cup chopped walnuts

Instructions:
1. Place a bowl with the cottage cheese in it.
2. Add chopped walnuts and fresh pineapple slices on top.
3. Dish out and savor!

CHIA SEED PUDDING WITH BERRIES:

Ingredients:
- 1/4 cup chia seeds
- 1 cup unsweetened almond milk
- 1/2 tsp vanilla extract
- 1 tbsp honey
- 1/2 cup mixed fresh berries (such as blueberries, raspberries, and strawberries)

Instructions:
1. Combine the chia seeds, almond milk, honey, and vanilla essence in a dish.
2. Allow the mixture to settle for 5 to 10 minutes so that the chia seeds may absorb the liquid and the mixture thickens.
3. Add a variety of fresh berries to a bowl with the chia seed pudding.
4. Dish out and savor!

VEGGIE BREAKFAST BURRITO WITH BLACK BEANS AND SALSA:

Ingredients:

- 1 whole grain tortilla
- 2 eggs
- 1/4 cup chopped onion
- 1/4 cup chopped bell pepper
- 1/4 cup black beans, drained and rinsed
- 1/4 cup salsa
- Salt and pepper to taste
- 1 tbsp olive oil

Instructions:

1. Beat the eggs with salt and pepper in a small bowl.
2. In a skillet over medium heat, warm the olive oil.
3. Add the bell pepper and onion, cut, and sauté for 2–3 minutes or until softened.
4. Add the beaten eggs and black beans to the skillet, heat, and scramble the eggs while stirring constantly.
5. Microwave the tortilla for 10 seconds to preheat it.
6. After adding the egg and black bean mixture, spoon the salsa on top of the tortilla.
7. Wrap the tortilla into a burrito, then warmly serve.

TUNA SALAD ON WHOLE GRAIN TOAST:

Ingredients:

- 1 can tuna, drained and flaked
- 1/4 cup chopped celery
- 1/4 cup chopped red onion

- 2 tbsp plain Greek yogurt
- 1 tbsp Dijon mustard
- Salt and pepper to taste
- 2 slices of whole-grain toast
- Optional toppings: lettuce, sliced tomato

Instructions:

1. Combine the tuna, diced celery and red onion, Greek yogurt, Dijon mustard, salt, and pepper in a mixing dish.
2. Toast the whole-grain bread to the level of crispness that you choose.
3. Top the toast with the tuna salad mixture.
4. If desired, top with extras like lettuce and tomato slices.
5. Present and savor!

BAKED SWEET POTATO WITH GREEK YOGURT AND BERRIES:

Ingredients:

- 1 medium sweet potato
- 1/2 cup Greek yogurt
- 1/2 cup mixed fresh berries (such as blueberries, raspberries, and strawberries)
- 1 tbsp honey

Instructions:

1. Set oven temperature to 400°F (200°C).
2. After washing, stab the sweet potato several times with a fork.
3. Arrange the sweet potatoes on a baking sheet and bake for 45 to 60 minutes or until they are soft and cooked.

4. Cut the sweet potato in half lengthwise after allowing it to cool for a few minutes.
5. Place a dollop of Greek yogurt on each half of a sweet potato.
6. Add fresh mixed berries on top and sprinkle honey over them.
7. Plate and savor!

TURKEY AND EGG BREAKFAST SANDWICH ON WHOLE GRAIN ENGLISH MUFFIN:

Ingredients:
- 1 whole grain English muffin, toasted
- 1 slice of low-sodium turkey breast
- 1 egg
- Salt and pepper to taste
- 1 slice of tomato
- 1 piece of avocado (optional)

Instructions:
1. Beat the egg with salt and pepper in a small basin.
2. Put a nonstick skillet on the stovetop at medium heat.
3. Stir in the beaten egg and cook it in the skillet until it is set, rotating once.
4. Toast the whole-wheat English muffin to the level of crispness that you choose.
5. Arrange the sliced tomato, cooked egg, low-sodium turkey breast, and avocado (if using) on the English muffin.
6. Dish out and savor!

OVERNIGHT OATS WITH ALMOND BUTTER AND BANANA:

Ingredients:
- 1/2 cup rolled oats
- 1/2 cup unsweetened almond milk
- 1 tbsp almond butter
- 1/2 banana, sliced
- 1 tbsp honey (optional)

Instructions:
1. Combine the rolled oats and almond milk in a bowl or Mason jar.
2. Add the banana slices and almond butter.
3. If desired, add honey on the top.
4. Cover and chill for the night.
5. Stir the oats in the morning and eat them!

BAKED EGG AND VEGGIE CUPS:

Ingredients:
- 4 eggs
- 1/4 cup chopped bell pepper
- 1/4 cup chopped onion
- 1/4 cup chopped zucchini
- Salt and pepper to taste
- Cooking spray

Instructions:
1. Set oven temperature to 350°F (175°C).
2. Spray cooking spray in a muffin pan.

3. Beat the eggs with salt and pepper in a mixing basin.
4. Add the minced onion, bell pepper, and zucchini.
5. Fill each cup in the muffin tin about 2/3 full with the egg and veggie mixture.
6. Bake the egg cups for 15 to 20 minutes until they are set and have a light golden brown top.
7. Please remove it from the muffin tin after letting it cool for a few minutes.
8. Plate hot, and savor!

APPLE CINNAMON QUINOA PORRIDGE:

Ingredients:
- 1/2 cup cooked quinoa
- 1/2 cup unsweetened almond milk
- 1/2 apple, chopped
- 1 tsp honey
- 1/4 tsp cinnamon

Instructions:
1. Combine the cooked quinoa and unsweetened almond milk in a small saucepan.
2. Include the cinnamon, honey, and apple chunks.
3. Combine, stir, and then bring to a boil.
4. Lower the heat to low and simmer the mixture for 5-7 minutes or until it has thickened.
5. Plate hot, and savor!

CHICKPEA AND VEGETABLE SCRAMBLE:

Ingredients:

- Two eggs
- 1/4 cup chopped onion
- 1/4 cup chopped bell pepper
- 1/4 cup chopped zucchini
- 1/4 cup canned chickpeas, drained and rinsed
- Salt and pepper to taste
- 1 tbsp olive oil

Instructions:

1. Beat the eggs with salt and pepper in a small bowl.
2. In a skillet over medium heat, warm the olive oil.
3. Include the diced onion, bell pepper, and zucchini. Sauté for 2-3 minutes or until the vegetables are just beginning to soften.
4. Add the chickpeas and stir to incorporate.
5. Pour the beaten eggs into the skillet and stir constantly when the eggs are cooked and scrambled.
6. Plate hot, and savor!

ZUCCHINI FRITTERS WITH POACHED EGGS:

Ingredients:

- 2 medium zucchinis, grated
- 1/4 cup all-purpose flour
- 1/4 teaspoon baking powder
- 1/4 teaspoon salt
- 1/4 teaspoon black pepper
- 2 eggs, beaten
- 1 tablespoon olive oil
- 2 poached eggs

Instructions:

1. Combine the beaten eggs, all-purpose flour, baking powder, salt, and pepper in a mixing bowl.
2. In a big nonstick skillet, heat the olive oil over medium-high heat.
3. Spoon the zucchini mixture into the skillet and flatten each one with a spatula as you go.
4. Cook for about 2 minutes on each side or until golden brown.
5. Place a poached egg on top of each zucchini cake before serving.

SMOKED SALMON BAGEL WITH CREAM CHEESE AND CUCUMBER:

Ingredients:

- 1 whole grain bagel
- 2 oz smoked salmon
- 2 tablespoons cream cheese
- 1/4 cucumber, sliced

Instructions:

1. Half the whole-grain bagel, then toast it to the desired crispness.
2. Apply cream cheese to the bagel's two halves.
3. Top one-half of the bagel with the smoked salmon.
4. Add the second half of the bagel and some sliced cucumber on top.
5. Present and savor!

MUSHROOM AND SPINACH FRITTATA:

Ingredients:

- 4 eggs
- 1/4 cup milk
- 1/4 cup chopped onion
- 1 cup sliced mushrooms
- 1 cup fresh spinach
- Salt and pepper to taste
- 1 tablespoon olive oil

Instructions:

1. Set the oven temperature to 375°F (190°C).

2. In a mixing bowl, stir the eggs, milk, salt, and pepper.
3. In a skillet over medium-high heat, warm the olive oil.
4. Add the minced onion and the sliced mushrooms, and cook for 2 to 3 minutes or until the mushrooms soften.
5. Include the new spinach in the skillet and mix well.
6. Add the egg mixture to the skillet and whisk just enough to combine.
7. Cook for 3 to 4 minutes or until the edges begin to set.
8. Place the skillet in the oven, and bake the frittata for 10 to 12 minutes or until the top is firm and browned.
9. Before slicing and serving, allow it cool for a few minutes.

EGG WHITE AND VEGETABLE WRAP:

Ingredients:
- 2 egg whites
- 1/4 cup chopped bell pepper
- 1/4 cup chopped onion
- 1/4 cup chopped zucchini
- Salt and pepper to taste
- 1 whole grain wrap

Instructions:
1. Whisk the egg whites with salt and pepper in a small bowl.
2. Put a nonstick skillet on the stovetop at medium heat.
3. Add the diced bell pepper, onion, and zucchini to the skillet and cook for 2 to 3 minutes or until the vegetables are just beginning to soften.
4. Once the eggs are cooked and scrambled, pour the whisked egg whites into the skillet and mix.

5. Microwave the whole-grain wrap for 10 seconds.
6. Place a spoonful of the egg and veggie mixture on the wrap, then fold it.
7. Plate and savor!

BERRY SMOOTHIE WITH CHIA SEEDS AND ALMOND MILK:

Ingredients:
- 1/2 cup mixed frozen berries
- 1/2 banana
- 1/2 cup unsweetened almond milk
- 1 tablespoon chia seeds
- 1 teaspoon honey (optional)

Instructions:
1. Place the mixed frozen berries, banana, unsweetened almond milk, chia seeds, and honey (if using) in a blender and blend until smooth.
2. Blend until creamy and smooth.
3. Transfer the smoothie to a glass, then sip it.

CHOCOLATE BANANA PROTEIN PANCAKES:

Ingredients:

- 1/2 cup whole wheat flour
- 1/4 cup chocolate protein powder
- 1/2 teaspoon baking powder
- 1/4 teaspoon salt
- 1 egg
- 1/2 banana, mashed
- 1/2 cup unsweetened almond milk
- 1/4 cup dark chocolate chips (optional)
- Cooking spray

Instructions:

1. Combine the whole wheat flour, chocolate protein powder, baking powder, and salt in a mixing dish.
2. Combine the egg, mashed banana, and unsweetened almond milk in a separate bowl.
3. Pour the wet ingredients into the dry ingredients to assemble the dish.
4. Include the dark chocolate chips when mixing.
5. Place a nonstick skillet over medium heat and coat it with cooking spray.
6. Add 1/4 cup of batter to the skillet and cook for 2 to 3 minutes or until bubbles form on the surface.
7. After flipping, cook the pancake for 1-2 minutes or until golden brown.
8. Continue by utilizing the remaining batter.
9. Add your choice of garnishes to the hot pancakes.

SHAKSHUKA WITH FETA CHEESE AND WHOLE GRAIN BREAD:

Ingredients:
- 1 tablespoon olive oil
- 1/2 onion, chopped
- 1 red bell pepper, chopped
- 2 garlic cloves, minced
- 1 teaspoon ground cumin
- 1 teaspoon paprika
- 1/4 teaspoon cayenne pepper
- 1 can (14.5 oz) diced tomatoes
- Four large eggs
- 1/4 cup crumbled feta cheese
- Salt and pepper to taste
- Whole grain bread for serving

Instructions:
1. Heat the olive oil in a large skillet over medium-low heat.
2. Add the onion and red bell pepper, chop them, and cook for 5 to 7 minutes or until tender.
3. Add the cayenne pepper, cumin, paprika, minced garlic, and sauté for another minute.
4. Combine everything in the skillet and add the can of diced tomatoes.
5. Let it simmer for 10 to 12 minutes or until the tomato sauce thickens.
6. After cracking the eggs within, cover the skillet.
7. Cook for 5-7 minutes until the egg whites are set but the yolks are still runny.
8. Sprinkle salt and pepper on top and add crumbled feta cheese.

9. Serve the shakshuka with warm whole-grain bread on the side.

EGG AND AVOCADO SALAD ON WHOLE GRAIN TOAST:

Ingredients:

- Two eggs, hard-boiled and chopped
- 1 avocado, diced
- 1/4 cup chopped cucumber
- 1/4 cup chopped tomato
- 1 tablespoon chopped fresh cilantro
- Salt and pepper to taste
- 2 slices whole grain bread

Instructions:

1. Combine the diced avocado, cucumber, tomato, and chopped cilantro in a mixing dish.
2. To taste, add salt and pepper to the food.
3. Toast the whole grain bread pieces.
4. Top the toast with the egg and avocado salad and serve.

BLUEBERRY PROTEIN WAFFLES:

Ingredients:

- 1 cup whole wheat flour
- 1/4 cup vanilla protein powder
- 1 teaspoon baking powder
- 1/4 teaspoon salt
- 1 egg
- 1 cup unsweetened almond milk
- 1/2 cup blueberries
- Cooking spray

Instructions:

1. In a mixing bowl, stir together the whole wheat flour, vanilla protein powder, baking powder, and salt.
2. Combine the egg and unsweetened almond milk in another bowl.
3. Combine the dry components with the wet ingredients by pouring them into each other.
4. Add the blueberries and stir.
5. Spray cooking spray on a waffle iron and preheat it.
6. Spoon the batter into the waffle iron and cook it following the directions provided by the manufacturer.
7. Carry on by using the leftover batter.
8. Top the hot waffles with your preferred toppings.

CAULIFLOWER RICE AND EGG BREAKFAST BOWL:

Ingredients:

- 1 cup cauliflower rice
- 1 tablespoon olive oil
- 1/4 cup chopped onion
- 1/4 cup chopped bell pepper
- 1/4 cup chopped zucchini
- 1/4 teaspoon salt
- 1/4 teaspoon black pepper
- 1/4 teaspoon garlic powder
- 2 eggs, scrambled
- 1 tablespoon chopped fresh parsley

Instructions:

1. Heat the olive oil in a nonstick skillet over medium-high heat.
2. Add the diced bell pepper, zucchini, onion, and sauté for 5 to 7 minutes, or until the vegetables soften.
3. Add the garlic powder, salt, and black pepper to the skillet and cauliflower rice.
4. Cook the cauliflower rice for 3–4 minutes or until it is cooked and slightly browned.
5. Scramble the eggs in another pan.
6. Split the mixture of cauliflower and rice into two bowls.
7. Add scrambled eggs and freshly cut parsley to the top of each bowl.
8. Present heat.

CHAPTER 5: RECIPES FOR LUNCH

GRILLED CHICKEN SALAD WITH MIXED GREENS AND VEGGIES:

Ingredients:

- 1 boneless, skinless chicken breast
- 4 cups mixed greens
- 1/2 cup cherry tomatoes, halved
- 1/2 cup sliced cucumber
- 1/4 cup sliced red onion
- 1/4 cup sliced almonds
- 2 tablespoons balsamic vinegar
- 1 tablespoon olive oil
- Salt and pepper to taste

Instructions:

1. Turn the heat to medium-high on a grill or grill pan.
2. Salt and pepper the chicken breast, then grill it for 6-7 minutes per side or until done.
3. After giving the chicken some time to rest, cut it into strips.
4. Combine the mixed greens, cherry tomatoes, cucumber slices, red onion, and almonds in a mixing dish.
5. Combine the balsamic vinegar, olive oil, and a dash of salt and pepper in a small bowl.
6. Pour the salad with the dressing and toss to combine.
7. Place the chicken breast slices on top of the salad and serve.

BROILED SALMON WITH ROASTED VEGETABLES:

Ingredients:

- 4 salmon fillets
- 4 cups mixed vegetables (such as broccoli, bell peppers, and zucchini), chopped
- 2 tablespoons olive oil
- 2 cloves garlic, minced
- 1 teaspoon dried oregano
- Salt and pepper to taste

Instructions:

1. Set the broiler to high heat.
2. Arrange the chopped veggies on a baking sheet lined with parchment paper.
3. In a small bowl, combine the olive oil, minced garlic, dried oregano, and a dash of salt and pepper.
4. Drizzle the vegetables with the dressing and toss to coat.
5. Top the vegetables with the salmon fillets.
6. Broil for 8 to 10 minutes or until the veggies are soft and slightly browned and the salmon is done.
7. Present hot.

TUNA SALAD WITH LEAFY GREENS AND CHERRY TOMATOES:

Ingredients:

- 2 cans tuna, drained
- 1/4 cup chopped celery
- 1/4 cup chopped red onion
- 1/4 cup chopped dill pickles
- 1/4 cup plain Greek yogurt
- 2 tablespoons Dijon mustard
- 1 tablespoon lemon juice
- Salt and pepper to taste
- 4 cups mixed greens
- 1/2 cup cherry tomatoes, halved

Instructions:

1. Mix the drained tuna with the celery, red onion, dill pickles, plain Greek yogurt, Dijon mustard, lemon juice, salt, and pepper in a mixing dish.
2. Stir to blend thoroughly.
3. Combine the mixed greens, cherry tomatoes, a drizzle of olive oil, and a sprinkle of salt and pepper in a different mixing bowl.
4. Distribute the cherry tomatoes and mixed greens among the four dishes.
5. Place a serving of tuna salad on top of each plate.
6. Offer chilled.

TURKEY AND AVOCADO WRAP WITH WHOLE WHEAT TORTILLA:

Ingredients:

- 1 whole wheat tortilla
- 4 oz. sliced turkey breast
- 1/2 avocado, sliced
- 1/4 cup shredded lettuce
- 2 slices tomato
- 1 tablespoon mayonnaise
- Salt and pepper to taste

Instructions:

1. The whole wheat tortilla should be placed on a flat surface.
2. Cover the tortilla with mayonnaise.
3. Arrange tomato, lettuce, avocado, and sliced turkey breast slices on the mayonnaise.
4. To taste, add salt and pepper to the dish.
5. After cutting the tortilla in half, roll it tightly.
6. Serve right away.

LENTIL SOUP WITH CARROTS AND CELERY:

Ingredients:

- 1 tablespoon olive oil
- 1 onion, chopped
- 2 garlic cloves, minced
- 2 carrots, chopped
- 2 celery stalks, chopped
- 1 cup dry lentils, rinsed and drained
- 4 cups vegetable broth
- 1/2 teaspoon ground cumin
- Salt and pepper to taste

Instructions:

1. In a big pot over medium-high heat, warm the olive oil.
2. Include the minced garlic, diced onion, and sauté for 2–3 minutes or until softened.
3. Stir in the chopped carrots and celery, and cook for 5-7 minutes or until they soften.
4. Fill the pot with the dry lentils, vegetable stock, and ground cumin.
5. After bringing the soup to a boil, lower the heat to a simmer and cook the lentils for 30-35 minutes or until soft.
6. Add salt and pepper to taste and season the soup.
7. Present hot.

GRILLED SHRIMP SKEWERS WITH QUINOA SALAD:

Ingredients:

- 1 lb. large shrimp, peeled and deveined
- 1/4 cup olive oil
- 2 garlic cloves, minced
- 1 tablespoon chopped fresh parsley
- 1 tablespoon chopped fresh basil
- Salt and pepper to taste
- 1 cup cooked quinoa
- 1/2 cup cherry tomatoes, halved
- 1/2 cup diced cucumber
- 1/4 cup crumbled feta cheese
- 2 tablespoons lemon juice
- 1 tablespoon olive oil
- Salt and pepper to taste

Instructions:

1. Turn the heat to medium-high on a grill or grill pan.
2. Combine the olive oil, minced garlic, fresh parsley, basil, salt, and pepper in a mixing bowl.
3. Skewer the shrimp, then brush them with the marinade.
4. Grill the shrimp skewers until pink and slightly browned, about 2 to 3 minutes per side.
5. Combine the cooked quinoa, diced cucumber, feta cheese, lemon juice, olive oil, salt, and pepper in a different mixing dish.
6. Combine by tossing.
7. Include the quinoa salad alongside the grilled shrimp skewers.

GRILLED TOFU AND VEGETABLE KEBABS:

Ingredients:

- 1 block firm tofu, drained and cut into cubes
- 1 red bell pepper, cut into chunks
- 1 green bell pepper, cut into chunks
- 1 yellow squash, sliced
- 1 zucchini, sliced
- 1 red onion, cut into chunks
- 2 tablespoons olive oil
- 2 garlic cloves, minced
- 1 teaspoon dried oregano
- Salt and pepper to taste
- Wooden or metal skewers

Instructions:

1. Turn the heat to medium-high on a grill or grill pan.
2. Combine the olive oil, minced garlic, dried oregano, salt, and pepper in a mixing dish.
3. Thread the skewers with the tofu pieces and chopped vegetables.
4. Apply the olive oil mixture to the kebabs.
5. Grill the kebabs on each side for 6 to 8 minutes until the tofu is browned and the vegetables are slightly scorched.
6. Present hot.

MIXED VEGETABLE STIR-FRY WITH BROWN RICE:

Ingredients:

- 1 cup brown rice
- 2 cups water
- 2 tablespoons olive oil
- 2 garlic cloves, minced
- 1 red bell pepper, sliced
- 1 green bell pepper, sliced
- 1 yellow onion, sliced
- 1 zucchini, sliced
- 1 yellow squash, sliced
- Salt and pepper to taste
- 2 tablespoons soy sauce

Instructions:

1. Combine the water and brown rice in a saucepan.
2. After bringing the rice to a boil, boil the heat and let it simmer for 40 to 45 minutes or until it is soft.
3. Heat the olive oil over medium-high heat in a sizable skillet or wok.
4. Include the minced garlic and cook for a few minutes or until fragrant.
5. Stir-fry the onion and bell pepper slices in the skillet for 3–4 minutes or until they soften.
6. Include the yellow squash and zucchini slices in the skillet and stir-fry for 2 to 3 minutes or until all the vegetables are soft.
7. Add salt and pepper to taste and season the vegetables.
8. Add the soy sauce, stir, and simmer for one more minute.

9. Spoon the brown rice on top of the mixed vegetable stir-fry.

CHICKEN AND VEGETABLE SOUP:

Ingredients:
- 1 tablespoon olive oil
- 1 onion, chopped
- 2 garlic cloves, minced
- 2 carrots, chopped
- 2 celery stalks, chopped
- 4 cups chicken broth
- 2 cups cooked shredded chicken
- 1 cup frozen peas
- 1 cup frozen corn
- Salt and pepper to taste
- Chopped fresh parsley for garnish

Instructions:
1. In a big pot over medium-high heat, warm the olive oil.
2. Include the minced garlic, diced onion, and sauté for 2–3 minutes or until softened.
3. Stir in the chopped carrots and celery, and cook for 5-7 minutes or until they soften.
4. Stir in the chicken broth and bring the mixture to a boil.
5. Stir the shredded chicken, frozen peas, and frozen corn in the pot.
6. Lower the heat to a low setting and boil the soup for 15 to 20 minutes or until the vegetables are soft.
7. Add salt and pepper to taste and season the soup.
8. Garnish with freshly cut parsley before serving hot.

BAKED SALMON WITH ASPARAGUS AND SWEET POTATO:

Ingredients:

- Four salmon fillets
- 1 lb. asparagus, trimmed
- 2 sweet potatoes, peeled and chopped
- 2 tablespoons olive oil
- 2 cloves garlic, minced
- Salt and pepper to taste

Instructions:

1. Turn on the oven to 400°F.
2. Arrange the chopped sweet potatoes and trimmed asparagus on a baking sheet lined with parchment paper.
3. Combine the olive oil, minced garlic, and a little salt and pepper in a small bowl.
4. Drizzle the vegetables with the dressing and toss to coat.
5. Top the vegetables with the salmon fillets.
6. Bake the salmon for 15 to 20 minutes or until it is done and the vegetables are soft.
7. Present hot.

CHICKPEA SALAD WITH CUCUMBERS AND TOMATOES:

Ingredients:

- 2 cans chickpeas, drained and rinsed
- 1 cucumber, chopped
- 1 pint cherry tomatoes, halved
- 1/4 cup chopped red onion
- 1/4 cup chopped fresh parsley

- 2 tablespoons olive oil
- 2 tablespoons lemon juice
- Salt and pepper to taste

Instructions:

1. Combine the rinsed and drained chickpeas, diced cucumber, cherry tomatoes cut in half, chopped red onion, and chopped fresh parsley in a mixing dish.
2. Combine the olive oil, lemon juice, salt, and pepper in a small bowl.
3. Drizzle the chickpea salad with the dressing and toss to combine.
4. Offer chilled.

TURKEY AND VEGETABLE CHILI:

Ingredients:
- 1 tablespoon olive oil
- 1 onion, chopped
- 2 garlic cloves, minced
- 1 lb. ground turkey
- 2 bell peppers, chopped
- 2 zucchinis, chopped
- 2 cans diced tomatoes
- 2 cans kidney beans, drained and rinsed
- 1 tablespoon chili powder
- One teaspoon of ground cumin
- Salt and pepper to taste

Instructions:

1. In a big pot over medium-high heat, warm the olive oil.
2. Include the minced garlic, diced onion, and sauté for 2–3 minutes or until softened.
3. Add the ground turkey to the pot and simmer until browned and cooked, breaking up the meat with a spoon.
4. Stir in the diced bell peppers and zucchini, and cook for 5 to 7 minutes or until the vegetables soften.
5. Add the kidney beans, chili powder, ground cumin, drained and rinsed diced tomatoes, and a dash of salt and pepper to the saucepan.
6. Simmer the chili for 15 to 20 minutes or until the vegetables are soft and the flavors are well-balanced.
7. Add salt and pepper to taste and season the chili.
8. Present heat.

GRILLED CHICKEN AND VEGETABLE KABOBS:

Ingredients:

- 1 lb. boneless, skinless chicken breast, cut into cubes
- 1 red bell pepper, cut into chunks
- 1 green bell pepper, cut into chunks
- 1 zucchini, sliced
- 1 yellow squash, sliced
- 1 red onion, cut into chunks
- 2 tablespoons olive oil
- 2 garlic cloves, minced
- 1 teaspoon dried thyme
- Salt and pepper to taste
- Wooden or metal skewers

Instructions:
1. Turn the heat to medium-high on a grill or grill pan.
2. Combine the olive oil, minced garlic, dried thyme, salt, and pepper in a mixing dish.
3. Thread the skewers with the diced vegetables and chicken.
4. Apply the olive oil mixture to the kebabs.
5. Grill the kebabs on each side for 6 to 8 minutes until the chicken is cooked and the veggies are just beginning to brown.
6. Present hot.

BROILED FISH WITH STEAMED VEGETABLES:

Ingredients:
- Four fish fillets (such as salmon or tilapia)
- 1 lb. mixed vegetables (such as broccoli, carrots, and green beans), trimmed and cut into bite-size pieces
- 2 tablespoons olive oil
- 2 garlic cloves, minced
- Salt and pepper to taste

Instructions:
1. Set the broiler to high heat.
2. Arrange the fish fillets on a baking sheet lined with parchment paper.
3. Combine the olive oil, minced garlic, salt, and pepper in a small bowl.
4. Drizzle the fish fillets with the dressing and toss to coat.
5. Add a few tablespoons of water and arrange the mixed veggies in a steamer basket or microwave-safe dish.

When the vegetables are soft but slightly crunchy, microwave them for two to three minutes or steam them on the stovetop.
6. Position the steamed veggies around the fish fillets on the baking sheet.
7. Broil the veggies and fish for 6 to 8 minutes or until the vegetables are slightly browned, and the fish is cooked through.
8. Present heat.

BLACK BEAN AND VEGETABLE ENCHILADAS:

Ingredients:
- 2 tablespoons olive oil
- 1 onion, chopped
- 2 garlic cloves, minced
- 1 red bell pepper, chopped
- 1 zucchini, chopped
- 1 cup cooked black beans, drained and rinsed
- 1 tablespoon chili powder
- 1 teaspoon ground cumin
- Salt and pepper to taste
- Eight corn tortillas
- 1 cup enchilada sauce
- 1 cup shredded Monterey Jack cheese
- Chopped fresh cilantro for garnish

Instructions:
1. Set the oven's temperature to 350°F.
2. In a big skillet over medium-high heat, warm the olive oil.

3. Include the minced garlic, diced onion, and sauté for 2 to 3 minutes or until softened.
4. Stir in the diced red bell pepper and zucchini, and cook for 5 to 7 minutes or until the vegetables start softening.
5. Stir together the black beans cooked with the chili powder, ground cumin, salt, and pepper in the skillet.
6. Microwave or grill the corn tortillas to a warm temperature.
7. Fill the bottom of a 9x13-inch baking dish with a few tablespoons of enchilada sauce.
8. Spoon a little of the veggie and black bean mixture into each tortilla before rolling it up.
9. Set the tort on a plate.

TURKEY BURGER WITH WHOLE WHEAT BUN AND SIDE SALAD:

Ingredients:

- 1 lb. ground turkey
- 1/4 cup finely chopped onion
- 2 tablespoons chopped fresh parsley
- 1 tablespoon Dijon mustard
- 1/2 teaspoon salt
- 1/4 teaspoon black pepper
- 4 whole wheat burger buns
- 4 slices tomato
- 4 leaves lettuce
- 1/2 cup mixed greens
- 1/2 cup sliced cucumber
- 1/2 cup sliced carrots
- 1/4 cup balsamic vinaigrette

Instructions:

1. Combine the ground turkey, finely chopped onion, fresh parsley, Dijon mustard, salt, and pepper in a mixing bowl. Combine thoroughly after mixing.
2. Form the turkey mixture into patties by dividing it into 4 equal portions.
3. Turn the heat to medium-high on a grill or grill pan.
4. To cook the turkey patties, grill them for 6-7 minutes on each side.
5. Place the turkey burgers on whole-wheat buns and top each with a lettuce leaf and a tomato slice.
6. Combine the mixed greens, thinly sliced cucumber, thinly sliced carrots, and balsamic vinaigrette in a different mixing bowl. Coat by tossing.
7. Put the side salad on the table with the turkey burgers.

SHRIMP AND VEGETABLE STIR-FRY WITH BROWN RICE:

Ingredients:

- 1 lb. shrimp, peeled and deveined
- 1 red bell pepper, sliced
- 1 green bell pepper, sliced
- 1 zucchini, sliced
- 1 yellow squash, sliced
- 1 onion, sliced
- 2 tablespoons olive oil
- 2 garlic cloves, minced
- Salt and pepper to taste
- 2 cups cooked brown rice

Instructions:

1. Heat the olive oil over medium-high heat in a big skillet or wok.
2. After a minute or two, add the minced garlic and cook until fragrant.
3. Stir-fry the onion, bell pepper, zucchini, and yellow squash slices in the skillet for 5 to 7 minutes or until they soften.
4. Stir-fry the peeled and deveined shrimp for 2 to 3 minutes or until they are pink and done.
5. Add salt and pepper to taste and season the stir-fry.
6. Spoon the cooked brown rice with shrimp and vegetables on top of the stir-fry.

LENTIL AND VEGETABLE CURRY:

Ingredients:

- 1 cup dry red lentils
- 2 tbsp vegetable oil
- 1 onion, chopped
- 2 garlic cloves, minced
- 1 tbsp grated fresh ginger
- 1 tsp ground cumin
- 1 tsp ground coriander
- 1/2 tsp ground turmeric
- 1/2 tsp ground cinnamon
- 1/2 tsp cayenne pepper
- 1 large sweet potato, peeled and diced
- 2 carrots, peeled and diced
- 1 red bell pepper, seeded and diced
- 1 zucchini, diced

- 1 can diced tomatoes, undrained
- 2 cups vegetable broth
- Salt and black pepper, to taste
- Chopped fresh cilantro for garnish
- Cooked rice or naan bread for serving

Instructions:

1. Use a fine-mesh strainer to rinse the lentils, then set them aside.
2. Heat the oil over medium heat in a big saucepan or Dutch oven. Add the onion and cook for about 5 minutes or until tender and transparent.
3. Add the ginger and garlic, and cook for an additional two minutes.
4. Add the spices and whisk to incorporate the cumin, coriander, turmeric, cinnamon, and cayenne.
5. Add the diced tomatoes (and their juice), zucchini, bell pepper, sweet potato, and vegetable broth. Stir to incorporate.
6. Include the lentils and blend by stirring.
7. Bring the mixture to a boil, lower the heat to a simmer, cover it, and cook for 30 to 40 minutes, or until the lentils and veggies are cooked.
8. To taste, add salt and black pepper.
9. Serve the curry hot, with rice or naan bread on the side and fresh cilantro as a garnish.

GRILLED PORTOBELLO MUSHROOM AND VEGGIE WRAP:

Ingredients:

- 2 large Portobello mushroom caps, stems removed
- 1 red bell pepper, sliced
- 1 zucchini, sliced
- 1 yellow squash, sliced
- 2 tablespoons olive oil
- 2 garlic cloves, minced
- Salt and pepper to taste
- 4 whole wheat wraps
- 1/2 cup hummus
- 1/2 cup mixed greens

Instructions:

1. Turn the heat to medium-high on a grill or grill pan.
2. Combine the olive oil, minced garlic, salt, and pepper in a mixing dish.
3. Apply the olive oil mixture to the sliced veggies and Portobello mushroom caps.
4. Grill the mushroom caps and veggies on each side for 5 to 7 minutes until they are soft and slightly browned.
5. To assemble the wraps, spread some hummus on each and top with grilled veggies, mixed greens, and a grilled Portobello mushroom cap.
6. To serve, carefully roll the wraps and cut them in half.

BAKED CHICKEN WITH GREEN BEANS AND CARROTS:

Ingredients:

- 4 boneless, skinless chicken breasts
- 1 lb. green beans, trimmed
- 2 cups baby carrots
- 2 tablespoons olive oil
- 2 garlic cloves, minced
- Salt and pepper to taste

Instructions:

1. Turn on the oven to 400°F.
2. Arrange the chicken breasts on a baking sheet lined with parchment paper.
3. Combine the olive oil, minced garlic, salt, and pepper in a mixing dish.
4. After coating the chicken breasts with the dressing, drizzle it over them.
5. Position the baby carrots and green beans around the chicken breasts on the baking pan.
6. Bake the chicken and vegetables for 25 to 30 minutes or until the chicken is cooked.
7. Present hot.

TOFU AND VEGETABLE STIR-FRY WITH BROWN RICE:

Ingredients:

- 1 lb. extra-firm tofu, drained and cut into cubes
- 1 red bell pepper, sliced
- 1 zucchini, sliced
- 1 yellow squash, sliced
- 1 onion, sliced
- 2 tablespoons olive oil
- 2 garlic cloves, minced
- Salt and pepper to taste
- 2 cups cooked brown rice

Instructions:

1. Heat the olive oil over medium-high heat in a big skillet or wok.
2. Add the cubed, drained tofu to the skillet and stir-fry for 5 to 7 minutes or until crispy and lightly browned.
3. Take the tofu out of the pan and place it aside.
4. Add the onion, red bell pepper, zucchini, and yellow squash slices to the skillet and stir-fry for 5 to 7 minutes or until the vegetables start softening.
5. Add the cooked tofu back to the skillet and mix well.
6. Add salt and pepper to taste and season the stir-fry.
7. Spoon the cooked brown rice over the tofu and veggie stir-fry.

SPINACH AND FETA STUFFED CHICKEN BREAST:

Ingredients:

- 4 boneless, skinless chicken breasts
- 2 cups packed spinach leaves
- 1/2 cup crumbled feta cheese
- 2 garlic cloves, minced
- Salt and pepper to taste
- 2 tablespoons olive oil

Instructions:

1. Set the oven to 375 degrees.
2. To make a pocket for the filling, split the side of each chicken breast.
3. In a mixing dish, combine the spinach leaves in a bag, the feta cheese that has been crumbled, and the minced garlic, salt, and pepper.
4. Stuff the spinach and feta mixture into each chicken breast using toothpicks to close the opening.
5. In a big skillet over medium-high heat, warm the olive oil.
6. To brown the chicken breasts, sear them for 2 to 3 minutes on each side.
7. Put the chicken breasts in a baking tray and simmer for 20 to 25 minutes.
8. Present heat.

ROASTED VEGETABLE AND CHICKPEA BOWL:

Ingredients:

- 1 lb. mixed vegetables (such as sweet potatoes, broccoli, and red onion), cut into bite-size pieces
- 1 can chickpeas, drained and rinsed
- 2 tablespoons olive oil
- 2 garlic cloves, minced
- Salt and pepper to taste
- 2 cups cooked quinoa
- 1/4 cup hummus
- Chopped fresh parsley for garnish

Instructions:

1. Turn on the oven to 400°F.
2. Arrange the mixed veggies and chickpeas on a baking sheet lined with parchment paper.
3. Combine the olive oil, minced garlic, salt, and pepper in a mixing dish.
4. Toss the veggies and chickpeas with the dressing after drizzling it over them.
5. After 20 to 25 minutes of roasting, the veggies and chickpeas should be soft and slightly browned.
6. Top the cooked quinoa with roasted veggies and chickpeas, a dollop of hummus, and fresh parsley that has been chopped.

GRILLED SHRIMP WITH BROWN RICE AND VEGETABLES:

Ingredients:

- 1 lb. shrimp, peeled and deveined
- 1 red bell pepper, sliced
- 1 zucchini, sliced
- 1 yellow squash, sliced
- 2 tablespoons olive oil
- 2 garlic cloves, minced
- Salt and pepper to taste
- 2 cups cooked brown rice

Instructions:

1. Turn the heat to medium-high on a grill or grill pan.
2. Combine the olive oil, minced garlic, salt, and pepper in a mixing dish.
3. Apply the olive oil mixture to the shrimp and chopped veggies.
4. Grill the shrimp and vegetables on each side for 5 to 7 minutes or until just cooked through.
5. Spoon the cooked brown rice over the grilled shrimp and vegetables.

TURKEY AND VEGETABLE SKEWERS WITH QUINOA SALAD:

Ingredients:

- 1 lb. turkey breast, cut into cubes
- 1 red bell pepper, sliced
- 1 zucchini, sliced
- 1 yellow squash, sliced
- 2 tablespoons olive oil
- 2 garlic cloves, minced
- Salt and pepper to taste
- 2 cups cooked quinoa
- 1/2 cup mixed greens
- 1/2 cup cherry tomatoes
- 1/4 cup chopped fresh parsley
- 1/4 cup lemon vinaigrette

Instructions:

1. Turn the heat to medium-high on a grill or grill pan.
2. Thread the sliced veggies and chunks of turkey breast onto skewers.
3. Combine the olive oil, minced garlic, salt, and pepper in a mixing dish.
4. Apply the olive oil mixture on the skewers of turkey and vegetables.
5. Grill the skewers on each side for 5-7 minutes, turning once, until the turkey is cooked and the vegetables start to brown.
6. In a different mixing dish, combine the cooked quinoa, mixed greens, cherry tomatoes, fresh parsley that has been chopped, and lemon vinaigrette. Coat by tossing.

7. Present the quinoa salad beside the grilled turkey and vegetables.

VEGETABLE AND TOFU CURRY:

Ingredients:

- 1 lb. extra-firm tofu, drained and cut into cubes
- 1 red bell pepper, sliced
- 1 zucchini, sliced
- 1 yellow squash, sliced
- 1 onion, sliced
- 2 tablespoons olive oil
- 2 garlic cloves, minced
- Salt and pepper to taste
- 1 can of coconut milk
- 2 tablespoons red curry paste
- 2 cups cooked brown rice

Instructions:

1. In a big pot over medium-high heat, warm the olive oil.
2. Add the cubed, drained tofu to the pot and cook for 5 to 7 minutes, until crispy and gently browned.
3. Take the tofu out of the cooker and leave it aside.
4. Add the sliced red bell pepper, yellow squash, zucchini, and onion to the pot and cook for 5 to 7 minutes or until the vegetables start softening.
5. Combine the coconut milk, red curry paste, salt, and pepper in a mixing dish.
6. Add the cooked tofu to the pot along with the vegetables, then cover everything with the coconut milk mixture.
7. Simmer the curry for 10 to 15 minutes, or until the veggies are fork-tender and the sauce slightly thickens.

8. Spoon the cooked brown rice over the curry with the vegetables and tofu.

BROILED FISH WITH VEGETABLE SKEWERS:

Ingredients:
- 4 fillets of fish (such as salmon or tilapia)
- 1 red bell pepper, sliced
- 1 zucchini, sliced
- 1 yellow squash, sliced
- 2 tablespoons olive oil
- 2 garlic cloves, minced
- Salt and pepper to taste

Instructions:
1. Start by turning the broiler high.
2. Skewers with sliced veggies should be used.
3. Combine the olive oil, minced garlic, salt, and pepper in a mixing dish.
4. Brush the olive oil mixture on the fish fillets and veggie skewers.
5. Arrange the fish fillets on a parchment-lined baking sheet.
6. To cook the fish fillets thoroughly, broil them for 6 to 8 minutes.
7. Arrange the veggie skewers on a different baking sheet and broil for 5 to 7 minutes or until soft and slightly browned.
8. Provide hot

BAKED CHICKEN WITH ROASTED VEGETABLES:

Ingredients:

- 4 boneless, skinless chicken breasts
- 1 lb. mixed vegetables (such as carrots, broccoli, and cauliflower), cut into bite-size pieces
- 2 tablespoons olive oil
- 2 garlic cloves, minced
- Salt and pepper to taste

Instructions:

1. Turn on the oven to 400°F.
2. Arrange the mixed veggies on a baking sheet lined with parchment paper.
3. Combine the olive oil, minced garlic, salt, and pepper in a mixing dish.
4. Drizzle the vegetables with the dressing and toss to coat.
5. Place the chicken breasts on top of the veg and top with any leftover dressing.
6. Bake the chicken and vegetables for 25 to 30 minutes or until the chicken is cooked.
7. Present hot.

QUINOA AND VEGETABLE STUFFED BELL PEPPERS:

Ingredients:

- 4 bell peppers, tops removed and seeds removed
- 1 cup cooked quinoa
- 1/2 cup diced tomatoes
- 1/2 cup diced zucchini
- 1/2 cup diced yellow squash

- 1/2 cup diced onion
- 2 garlic cloves, minced
- 1 tablespoon olive oil
- Salt and pepper to taste
- 1/4 cup shredded mozzarella cheese

Instructions:

1. Set the oven to 375 degrees.
2. Combine the cooked quinoa, diced tomatoes, yellow squash, zucchini, diced onion, minced garlic, olive oil, salt, and pepper in a mixing dish.
3. Stuff the quinoa and vegetable mixture into each bell pepper.
4. Put the stuffed bell peppers in an oven-safe dish and cover with foil.
5. Bake the bell peppers for 30-35 minutes or until soft.
6. Take the foil from the baking dish and top each stuffed bell pepper with shredded mozzarella cheese.
7. Bake the casserole in the oven for 5-7 minutes or until the cheese is melted and bubbling.
8. Present heat.

LENTIL AND VEGETABLE SOUP WITH WHOLE GRAIN BREAD:

Ingredients:

- 1 cup dried lentils, rinsed and drained
- 1 onion, diced
- 2 garlic cloves, minced
- 2 carrots, diced
- 2 celery stalks, diced
- 1 red bell pepper, diced
- 6 cups vegetable broth

- 1 teaspoon dried thyme
- Salt and pepper to taste
- Whole grain bread for serving

Instructions:

1. In a sizable pot, cook the minced garlic and diced onion for 2 to 3 minutes until aromatic.
2. Add the diced carrots, celery, and red bell pepper to the pot and cook for 5 to 7 minutes or until softened.
3. Fill the saucepan with the lentils that have been rinsed and drained, vegetable stock, dried thyme, salt, and pepper.
4. Bring the soup to a boil before lowering the heat.
5. Let the soup simmer for 25 to 30 minutes or until the veggies and the lentils are soft.
6. Provide a slice of whole-grain bread, hot lentil, and vegetable soup.

CHAPTER 6: RECIPES FOR DINNER

GRILLED CHICKEN WITH ROASTED VEGETABLES:

Ingredients:

- 4 boneless, skinless chicken breasts
- 1 lb. mixed vegetables (such as carrots, broccoli, and cauliflower), cut into bite-size pieces
- 2 tablespoons olive oil
- 2 garlic cloves, minced
- Salt and pepper to taste

Instructions:

1. Turn the grill's heat up to medium-high.
2. Combine the olive oil, minced garlic, salt, and pepper in a mixing dish.
3. Add the dressing to the mixture of veggies and toss to combine.
4. Cook the chicken breasts on the grill for 5 to 6 minutes on each side.
5. Roast the veggies in the oven at 400 degrees Fahrenheit for 15 to 20 minutes, or until soft and faintly browned, while the chicken grills.
6. Arrange the roasted veggies alongside the grilled chicken.

BROILED SALMON WITH QUINOA AND SPINACH SALAD:

Ingredients:

- 4 salmon fillets
- 2 tablespoons olive oil
- 2 garlic cloves, minced
- Salt and pepper to taste
- 2 cups cooked quinoa
- 2 cups baby spinach leaves
- 1/2 cup cherry tomatoes, halved
- 1/4 cup chopped fresh basil
- 1/4 cup lemon vinaigrette

Instructions:

1. Start by turning the broiler high.
2. Combine the olive oil, minced garlic, salt, and pepper in a mixing dish.
3. Use the olive oil mixture to brush the salmon fillets.
4. To ensure the salmon fillets are fully cooked, broil for 6 to 8 minutes.
5. In a different mixing dish, combine the cooked quinoa, baby spinach leaves, cherry tomatoes, fresh basil that has been chopped, and lemon vinaigrette. Coat by tossing.
6. Combine the quinoa and spinach salad with the grilled fish.

TURKEY MEATBALLS WITH ZUCCHINI NOODLES:

Ingredients:

- 1 lb. ground turkey
- 1 egg, beaten
- 1/2 cup whole wheat breadcrumbs
- 2 garlic cloves, minced
- Salt and pepper to taste
- 4 medium zucchinis, spiralized
- 2 tablespoons olive oil
- 2 garlic cloves, minced
- Salt and pepper to taste
- 1/4 cup grated parmesan cheese

Instructions:

1. Set the oven to 375 degrees.
2. In a mixing bowl, mash together the ground turkey, beaten egg, whole wheat breadcrumbs, minced garlic, salt, and pepper.
3. Shape the turkey mixture into meatballs using your hands.
4. Arrange the meatballs on a parchment-lined baking sheet and bake for 20 to 25 minutes or until done.
5. Spiralize the zucchini while the meatballs are baking.
6. Heat the olive oil in a large skillet over medium-high heat.
7. Stir in the minced garlic and cook for a few minutes or until fragrant.
8. Add the zoodles that have been spiralized to the skillet and cook for 2 to 3 minutes or until they start to soften.
9. To taste, sprinkle salt and pepper on the zucchini noodles.

10. Combine the sautéed zucchini noodles and parmesan cheese with the turkey meatballs.

BAKED COD WITH LEMON AND HERBS:

Ingredients:

- 4 cod fillets
- 2 tablespoons olive oil
- 2 garlic cloves, minced
- Salt and pepper to taste
- 1 lemon, thinly sliced
- 1/4 cup chopped fresh herbs (such as parsley, dill, and thyme)

Instructions:

1. Set the oven to 375 degrees.
2. Combine the olive oil, minced garlic, salt, and pepper in a mixing dish.
3. Apply the olive oil mixture to the cod fillets.
4. Put the fish fillets in a pan that has been parchment paper-lined for baking.
5. Add a few lemon slices and chopped fresh herbs to each fish fillet.
6. Bake the fish fillets in the oven for 12 to 15 minutes or until done.
7. Present hot.

LENTIL AND VEGETABLE STEW WITH BROWN RICE:

Ingredients:

- 1 cup dried lentils, rinsed and drained
- 1 onion, diced
- 2 garlic cloves, minced
- 2 carrots, diced
- 2 celery stalks, diced
- 1 red bell pepper, diced
- 6 cups vegetable broth
- 1 teaspoon dried thyme
- Salt and pepper to taste
- 2 cups cooked brown rice

Instructions:

1. In a sizable pot, cook the minced garlic and diced onion for 2 to 3 minutes until aromatic.
2. Add the diced carrots, celery, and red bell pepper to the pot and cook for 5 to 7 minutes or until softened.
3. Fill the saucepan with the lentils that have been rinsed and drained, vegetable stock, dried thyme, salt, and pepper.
4. Bring the stew to a boil before lowering the heat.
5. Simmer the stew for 25 to 30 minutes to cook the vegetables and soften the lentils.
6. Top the hot lentil and vegetable stew with a serving of brown rice that has been prepared.

GRILLED TOFU AND VEGETABLE KEBABS WITH BROWN RICE:

Ingredients:

- 1 block of firm tofu, cut into 1-inch cubes
- 2 bell peppers, cut into 1-inch pieces
- 1 zucchini, cut into 1-inch pieces
- 1 onion, cut into 1-inch pieces
- 2 tablespoons olive oil
- 2 garlic cloves, minced
- Salt and pepper to taste
- Wooden or metal skewers
- 2 cups cooked brown rice

Instructions:

1. Turn the grill's heat up to medium-high.
2. Combine the olive oil, minced garlic, salt, and pepper in a mixing dish.
3. Thread the skewers with the tofu, bell peppers, zucchini, and onion.
4. Apply the olive oil mixture on the skewers.
5. Grill the skewers on each side for 5-7 minutes until the tofu is heated and the vegetables are slightly browned.
6. Scoop cooked brown rice onto each plate and top with the hot, grilled tofu and vegetable kebabs.

PAN-SEARED SCALLOPS WITH ASPARAGUS AND QUINOA:

Ingredients:

- 1 lb. sea scallops
- 2 tablespoons olive oil
- Salt and pepper to taste
- 1 lb. asparagus, trimmed and cut into bite-size pieces
- 2 garlic cloves, minced
- 2 cups cooked quinoa
- 1/4 cup chopped fresh parsley
- 1 lemon, cut into wedges

Instructions:

1. After patting the sea scallops dry with a paper towel, salt and pepper them.
2. Heat the olive oil in a large skillet over medium-high heat.
3. Add the scallops to the skillet and cook for 2 to 3 minutes on each side until golden brown and fully cooked.
4. Take the scallops out of the skillet and place them on a plate.
5. Stir in the asparagus and minced garlic, and cook for 3 to 5 minutes or until the asparagus begins to tender.
6. Combine the cooked quinoa and freshly cut parsley in a mixing basin.
7. Distribute the asparagus and quinoa mixture among the four dishes.
8. Add a couple of pan-seared scallops and a squeeze of lemon juice to the top of each plate.

STUFFED BELL PEPPERS WITH GROUND TURKEY AND QUINOA:

Ingredients:
- 4 bell peppers, tops removed and seeded
- 1 lb. ground turkey
- 1 onion, diced
- 2 garlic cloves, minced
- 1 cup cooked quinoa
- 1 cup diced tomatoes
- 1/2 cup shredded mozzarella cheese
- Salt and pepper to taste

Instructions:
1. Set the oven to 375 degrees.
2. Brown and sauté the ground turkey in a big skillet over medium-high heat.
3. Stir in the minced garlic and onion dice, and cook for 2 to 3 minutes or until aromatic.
4. Stir together the diced tomatoes and cooked quinoa in the skillet.
5. Add salt and pepper to taste, and toss the turkey and quinoa together.
6. Place some of the mixtures inside each bell pepper.
7. Place the stuffed bell peppers in a baking dish and bake for 30-35 minutes or until the peppers are soft.
8. Top each stuffed pepper with shredded mozzarella cheese, then put them back in the oven for another 5 to 10 minutes to melt and bubble the cheese.
9. Present heat.

CHICKPEA AND VEGETABLE CURRY WITH WHOLE WHEAT NAAN

Ingredients:

- 2 tablespoons olive oil
- 1 onion, diced
- 2 garlic cloves, minced
- 2 teaspoons curry powder
- 1 teaspoon ground cumin
- 1 teaspoon ground coriander
- 1/4 teaspoon cayenne pepper
- 1 can chickpeas, rinsed and drained
- 2 cups diced vegetables (such as zucchini, eggplant, and bell peppers)
- 1 can dice tomatoes
- 1/4 cup chopped fresh cilantro
- Salt and pepper to taste
- Whole wheat naan for serving

Instructions:

1. Heat the olive oil in a big pot over medium-high heat.
2. Include the minced garlic and diced onion in the pot and cook for 2 to 3 minutes or until fragrant.
3. Stir together the curry powder, cumin, coriander, and cayenne pepper in the pot.
4. Fill the saucepan with the diced tomatoes, veggies, and rinsed, drained chickpeas.
5. Add salt and pepper to taste and season the mixture.
6. Once the vegetables are soft and the flavors are blended, cover the saucepan and simmer for 15 to 20 minutes.
7. Add the fresh cilantro, chopped.

8. Place some whole wheat naan on the side to serve the hot chickpea and vegetable curry.

SPAGHETTI SQUASH WITH TURKEY BOLOGNESE SAUCE:

Ingredients:

- 1 medium spaghetti squash, halved and seeded
- 1 lb. ground turkey
- 1 onion, diced
- 2 garlic cloves, minced
- 1 can dice tomatoes
- 1/2 cup tomato sauce
- 1 tablespoon dried basil
- 1 tablespoon dried oregano
- Salt and pepper to taste
- Grated Parmesan cheese for serving

Instructions:

1. Set the oven to 375 degrees.
2. Place the spaghetti squash, cut side up, on a baking sheet once it has been seeded and split in half.
3. Bake the spaghetti squash in the oven for 30 to 40 minutes or until it is fork-tender and easily punctured.
4. Brown and sauté the ground turkey in a big skillet over medium-high heat.
5. Add the minced garlic and onion to the skillet, and cook for 2 to 3 minutes or until fragrant.
6. Stir in the tomato sauce, dry basil, dried oregano, and diced tomatoes from the can.
7. Add salt and pepper to taste and season the turkey and tomato combination.

8. Simmer the turkey bolognese sauce for 10-15 minutes to bring the flavors together.
9. To make spaghetti squash, scrape it into strands with a fork and divide it among 4 plates.
10. Spoon enough turkey bolognese sauce on top of each serving of spaghetti squash.
11. Top each platter with grated Parmesan cheese and serve immediately.

GRILLED SHRIMP SKEWERS WITH AVOCADO AND TOMATO SALAD:

Ingredients:
- 1 lb. large shrimp, peeled and deveined
- 2 tablespoons olive oil
- Salt and pepper to taste
- 1 avocado, diced
- 1 pint cherry tomatoes, halved
- 1/4 cup chopped fresh cilantro
- 2 tablespoons lime juice

Instructions:
1. Turn the grill's heat up to medium-high.
2. Attach skewers with the deveined and peeled shrimp.
3. Season the shrimp skewers with salt and pepper and drizzle with olive oil.
4. Grill the shrimp skewers for two to three minutes on each side or until done and just starting to brown.
5. Combine the diced avocado, halved cherry tomatoes, fresh cilantro, and lime juice in a mixing dish.
6. Add salt and pepper to taste and season the avocado and tomato salad.

7. Place the avocado and tomato salad on the side and serve the grilled shrimp skewers hot.

BAKED CHICKEN WITH GREEN BEANS AND TOMATOES:

Ingredients:

- 4 boneless, skinless chicken breasts
- 2 tablespoons olive oil
- Salt and pepper to taste
- 1 lb. green beans, trimmed
- 1 pint cherry tomatoes, halved
- 2 garlic cloves, minced
- 1 teaspoon dried thyme
- 1 teaspoon dried rosemary

Instructions:

1. Set the oven to 375 degrees.
2. Put the chicken breasts in a baking dish, both skinless and boneless.
3. Sprinkle salt and pepper over the chicken breasts after brushing them with olive oil.
4. Place the chicken breasts in the baking dish and surround them with the trimmed green beans and cherry tomatoes.
5. Top the green beans and tomatoes with the minced garlic, dried thyme, and rosemary.
6. Bake the tomatoes, green beans, and chicken for 25 to 30 minutes or until the veggies are soft.
7. Present hot.

SEARED TUNA WITH SESAME GINGER SAUCE AND BROCCOLI:

Ingredients:

- 4 tuna steaks
- 2 tablespoons olive oil
- Salt and pepper to taste
- 2 cups broccoli florets
- 1/4 cup soy sauce
- 1/4 cup rice vinegar
- 2 tablespoons honey
- 2 tablespoons sesame oil
- 1 tablespoon grated fresh ginger
- 1 garlic clove, minced

Instructions:

1. To create the sesame ginger sauce, combine the soy sauce, rice vinegar, honey, sesame oil, grated fresh ginger, and chopped garlic in a small mixing bowl.
2. After patting the tuna steaks dry with a paper towel, season them with salt and pepper.
3. Heat the olive oil in a large skillet over medium-high heat.
4. Add the seasoned tuna steaks to the skillet and cook for 2 to 3 minutes on each side, depending on how you like your fish.
5. Take the tuna steaks out of the pan and place them aside.
6. Add the broccoli florets to the same skillet and cook for 3 to 5 minutes or until tender.
7. Distribute the sautéed broccoli and seared tuna steaks among the four dishes.
8. Top each tuna steak with the sesame ginger sauce and serve immediately.

VEGETABLE AND TOFU STIR-FRY WITH BROWN RICE:

Ingredients:

- 1 lb. extra-firm tofu, pressed and diced
- 2 tablespoons olive oil
- Salt and pepper to taste
- 2 cups chopped vegetables (such as bell peppers, broccoli, and carrots)
- 1 garlic clove, minced
- 1/4 cup soy sauce
- 2 tablespoons rice vinegar
- 1 tablespoon honey
- 1 teaspoon cornstarch
- 2 cups cooked brown rice

Instructions:

1. Heat the olive oil in a large skillet over medium-high heat.
2. Add salt and pepper to the skillet before adding the diced tofu.
3. Sauté the tofu for 5 to 7 minutes or until browned and just beginning to get crispy.
4. Take the tofu out of the skillet and place it to the side.
5. Include the diced veggies and minced garlic and cook for 5 to 7 minutes or until the vegetables are just beginning to soften.
6. To make the stir-fry sauce, combine the soy sauce, rice vinegar, honey, and cornstarch in a small mixing dish.
7. Cover the vegetables in the skillet with the stir-fry sauce and swirl to mix.
8. Stir the sauce into the skillet with the sautéed tofu.

9. Provide hot, overdone brown rice beside the stir-fry of vegetables and tofu.

GRILLED STEAK WITH ROASTED BRUSSELS SPROUTS AND SWEET POTATO WEDGES

Ingredients:
- 4 boneless beef steaks
- 2 tablespoons olive oil
- Salt and pepper to taste
- 1 lb. Brussels sprouts, trimmed and halved
- 2 sweet potatoes, cut into wedges
- 2 garlic cloves, minced
- 1 teaspoon dried rosemary
- 1 teaspoon dried thyme

Instructions:
1. Turn the grill's heat up to medium-high.
2. After brushing the boneless beef steaks with salt and pepper, they will be seasoned with olive oil.
3. Grill the steaks on each side for 3–4 minutes until they are well-browned and the doneness you choose.
4. Take the steaks from the grill and place them somewhere else to rest.
5. Set the oven to 400 Fahrenheit.
6. Combine the sweet potato wedges, minced garlic, dried rosemary, and dried thyme in a mixing dish.
7. Add olive oil to the vegetable combination and season with salt and pepper to suit.
8. Spread the vegetable mixture on a baking sheet in a single layer.
9. Roast the vegetables for 20 to 25 minutes or until they are soft and start caramelizing.

10. Present the hot, roasted Brussels sprouts and sweet potato wedges with the grilled steaks.

QUINOA STUFFED ACORN SQUASH WITH CRANBERRIES AND WALNUTS:

Ingredients:
- 2 acorn squash, halved and seeded
- 1 tablespoon olive oil
- Salt and pepper to taste
- 1 cup cooked quinoa
- 1/2 cup dried cranberries
- 1/2 cup chopped walnuts
- 1 tablespoon maple syrup
- 1/2 teaspoon ground cinnamon

Instructions:
1. Set the oven to 375 degrees.
2. Season the half acorn squash with salt and pepper after brushing it with olive oil.
3. Arrange the cut-side-down acorn squash halves on a baking sheet and roast for 30-35 minutes or until fork-tender.
4. Combine the cooked quinoa, chopped walnuts, dried cranberries, maple syrup, and ground cinnamon in a mixing dish.
5. Distribute the quinoa mixture among the two halves of cooked acorn squash.
6. Put the packed acorn squash halves back in the oven and heat for 10-15 minutes.
7. Warm the quinoa-filled acorn squash before serving.

BROILED FLOUNDER WITH RATATOUILLE:

Ingredients:

- 4 flounder fillets
- 2 tablespoons olive oil
- Salt and pepper to taste
- 1 small eggplant, diced
- 1 small zucchini, diced
- 1 small yellow squash, diced
- 1 small onion, diced
- 1 red bell pepper, diced
- 2 garlic cloves, minced
- 1 tablespoon tomato paste
- 1/2 teaspoon dried oregano
- 1/2 teaspoon dried basil
- 1/2 teaspoon dried thyme

Instructions:

1. Start by turning the broiler high.
2. After brushing the flounder fillets with olive oil, they will be seasoned with salt and pepper.
3. Arrange the flounder fillets on a broiler pan and cook for 5 to 7 minutes.
4. Heat the olive oil in a large skillet over medium-high heat.
5. Add the diced eggplant, zucchini, yellow squash, onion, and red bell pepper to the skillet. Sauté for 5 to 7 minutes or until the vegetables start softening.
6. Add the tomato paste, dried thyme, dried basil, dried oregano, and dried oregano to the skillet and mix to incorporate.

7. Lower the heat to a low setting and simmer the ratatouille for 10 to 15 minutes or until the veggies are soft.
8. Place the ratatouille on the side and serve the hot broiled flounder.

LENTIL AND VEGETABLE SHEPHERD'S PIE WITH SWEET POTATO TOPPING:

Ingredients:
- 1 lb. sweet potatoes, peeled and cubed
- 2 tablespoons olive oil
- Salt and pepper to taste
- 1 small onion, diced
- 2 garlic cloves, minced
- 2 cups chopped vegetables (such as carrots, celery, and bell peppers)
- 1 cup cooked lentils
- 1 tablespoon tomato paste
- 1/2 teaspoon dried thyme
- 1/2 teaspoon paprika
- 1/2 cup vegetable broth

Instructions:
1. Set the oven to 375 degrees.
2. Cover the sweet potato cubes with water in a big pot and bring to a boil.
3. Lower the heat to medium-low, cover the saucepan, and simmer the sweet potato cubes for 15 to 20 minutes or until they are cooked.
4. After draining the sweet potato cubes, mash them with a fork or potato masher.
5. Taste-test, the salt and pepper, then add and set aside.

6. Heat the olive oil in a large skillet over medium heat.
7. Include the diced onion in the skillet and cook for 3 to 4 minutes or until the onion softens.
8. To the skillet, add the diced veggies and minced garlic. Cook for 5 to 7 minutes or until the vegetables are soft.
9. Stir together the cooked lentils, tomato paste, dried thyme, and paprika in the skillet.
10. Stir in the vegetable broth, and cook the lentil and vegetable combination for 5–7 minutes or until cooked through and slightly thickened.
11. Spoon the lentil and vegetable mixture evenly onto a sizable baking dish.
12. Cover the lentil and vegetable combination entirely with the mashed sweet potatoes by spoonfuls.
13. Bake the shepherd's pie in the oven for 25 to 30 minutes or until the mixture is heated and the sweet potato topping is gently browned.
1. Shepherd's pie with lentils and vegetables should be served hot.

BAKED EGGPLANT PARMESAN WITH WHOLE GRAIN PASTA:

Ingredients:

- 1 large eggplant, sliced into rounds
- 1 cup whole wheat panko breadcrumbs
- 1/2 cup grated Parmesan cheese
- 2 eggs, beaten
- 1/2 teaspoon dried oregano
- 1/2 teaspoon dried basil
- Salt and pepper to taste
- 1 jar (24 oz.) marinara sauce
- 8 oz. whole grain pasta

- 2 tablespoons chopped fresh parsley

Instructions:

1. Set the oven to 375 degrees.
2. Assemble the whole wheat panko breadcrumbs, grated Parmesan cheese, dried oregano, basil, salt, and pepper on a shallow plate.
3. After each eggplant round has been coated in the breadcrumb mixture, dip it in the beaten eggs.
4. Arrange the breaded eggplant rounds on a baking sheet and bake for 20 to 25 minutes or until crispy and golden brown.
5. Prepare the whole-grain pasta according to the package directions while the eggplant bakes.
6. Heat the marinara sauce to a warm consistency in a big pot over medium heat.
7. Could you take the baked eggplant out of the oven and set it aside?
8. Combine the warm marinara sauce with the cooked whole-grain pasta in a large mixing basin.
9. Spoon the spaghetti mixture onto a big baking pan.
10. Place the baked eggplant rounds on the pasta mixture, slightly overlapping.
11. Heat and lightly brown the eggplant parmesan in the oven for 10 to 15 minutes.
12. Top the hot eggplant parmesan with fresh parsley that has been chopped.

VEGETABLE FAJITAS WITH GUACAMOLE AND SALSA:

Ingredients:

- 1 large onion, sliced
- 1 red bell pepper, sliced
- 1 green bell pepper, sliced
- 1 yellow squash, sliced
- 1 zucchini, sliced
- 1 tablespoon olive oil
- Salt and pepper to taste
- 8 whole wheat tortillas
- 1 avocado, mashed
- 1/2 teaspoon cumin
- Juice of 1 lime
- Salt and pepper to taste
- 1/2 cup salsa

Instructions:

1. Heat the olive oil in a large skillet over medium-high heat.
2. Add the yellow squash, zucchini, red bell pepper, green bell pepper, and onion slices to the skillet and cook for 5 to 7 minutes or until the vegetables start softening.
3. Add salt and pepper to taste and season the vegetables.
4. Microwave or grill the whole-wheat tortillas to a warm temperature.
5. To make the guacamole, combine the mashed avocado, cumin, lime juice, salt, and pepper in a small mixing dish.
6. Arrange the warm whole wheat tortillas, guacamole, and salsa on the side with the hot sautéed vegetables.

CHICKEN AND VEGETABLE SKEWERS WITH CAULIFLOWER RICE:

Ingredients:

- 2 boneless, skinless chicken breasts cut into chunks
- 1 red bell pepper, cut into chunks
- 1 yellow bell pepper, cut into chunks
- 1 zucchini, sliced
- 1 onion, cut into chunks
- Salt and pepper to taste
- 2 tablespoons olive oil
- 1 head cauliflower, riced
- 1/4 cup chopped fresh parsley

Instructions:

1. Turn the grill's heat up to medium-high.
2. Alternately thread the onion chunks, bell pepper slices, zucchini slices, and chicken portions onto skewers.
3. Brush the skewers with olive oil and season with salt and pepper to taste.
4. Grill the skewers for 10 to 12 minutes, rotating them halfway through or until the chicken is cooked and the vegetables start to brown.
5. Pulse the cauliflower florets in a food processor until they resemble rice grains while the skewers roast.
6. Add the riced cauliflower to a big skillet that is already hot over medium-high heat.
7. Cook the cauliflower in a skillet for 5 to 7 minutes or until softened.
8. Add the fresh parsley that has been chopped and season the cauliflower rice with salt and pepper to taste.

9. Present the hot grilled chicken and veggie skewers with a side of cauliflower rice.

GRILLED PORK TENDERLOIN WITH GRILLED VEGETABLES AND BROWN RICE:

Ingredients:
- 1 lb. pork tenderloin
- 1 red bell pepper, sliced
- 1 yellow bell pepper, sliced
- 1 zucchini, sliced
- 1 onion, sliced
- 2 tablespoons olive oil
- Salt and pepper to taste
- 2 cups cooked brown rice
- 1/4 cup chopped fresh cilantro

Instructions:
1. Turn the grill's heat up to medium-high.
2. Drizzle some olive oil over the pork tenderloin and season it with salt and pepper to taste.
3. Grill the pork tenderloin for 15 to 20 minutes, flipping it once or twice or until it is done and just beginning to brown.
4. Toss the sliced red and yellow bell peppers, sliced zucchini, and sliced onion with the remaining olive oil and season with salt and pepper to taste while the pork tenderloin is grilling.
5. Grill the vegetables for 5 to 7 minutes or until slightly browned and softened.
6. Place the brown rice in a serving dish and add the grilled vegetables and pork tenderloin on the side.

7. Before serving, top the brown rice with fresh cilantro that has been chopped.

QUINOA STUFFED PEPPERS WITH BLACK BEANS AND CORN:

Ingredients:
- 4 bell peppers, halved and seeded
- 1 tablespoon olive oil
- 1 onion, chopped
- 2 cloves garlic, minced
- 1 cup cooked quinoa
- 1 can (15 oz.) black beans, drained and rinsed
- 1 cup frozen corn, thawed
- 1/2 teaspoon ground cumin
- Salt and pepper to taste
- 1 cup shredded cheddar cheese

Instructions:
1. Set the oven to 375 degrees.
2. Arrange the bell peppers in a baking dish, which have been seeded and cut in half.
3. Heat the olive oil in a large skillet over medium heat.
4. Add the chopped onion and garlic to the skillet and cook for 2 to 3 minutes or until the onion is tender.
5. Add the frozen corn, black beans, drained and rinsed quinoa, ground cumin, salt, and pepper.
6. Fill the bell pepper halves to the brim with the quinoa mixture.
7. Place foil over the baking dish and bake for 25 to 30 minutes.

8. Take off the foil, top the stuffed peppers with the shredded cheddar cheese, and bake for 10-15 minutes or until the cheese is melted and bubbling.
9. Immediately serve the filled peppers.

ZUCCHINI NOODLES WITH SHRIMP AND TOMATO SAUCE:

Ingredients:

- 4 medium zucchini, spiralized
- 1 tablespoon olive oil
- 1 lb. medium shrimp, peeled and deveined
- 2 cloves garlic, minced
- 1 can (15 oz.) diced tomatoes
- 1/2 teaspoon dried basil
- 1/2 teaspoon dried oregano
- Salt and pepper to taste
- 1/4 cup chopped fresh parsley

Instructions:

1. Heat the olive oil in a large skillet over medium-high heat.
2. Add the deveined and peeled shrimp to the skillet and cook for 2 to 3 minutes or until pink and curled.
3. Take the cooked shrimp from the skillet and place them on a plate.
4. Stir in the minced garlic and cook for a few minutes or until fragrant.
5. Add salt, pepper, dried oregano, dry basil, and the diced tomatoes from the can with their juice.
6. Simmer the tomato sauce for 10 to 12 minutes or until it thickens slightly.

7. Spiralize the zucchini and leave aside while the tomato sauce is simmering.
8. After thickening the tomato sauce, add the chopped fresh parsley and the cooked shrimp back to the skillet.
9. Add the spiralized zucchini to the skillet and stir in the tomato sauce for 2 to 3 minutes or until the zucchini softens.
10. Arrange the shrimp and tomato sauce alongside the heated zucchini noodles.

GRILLED VEGETABLE AND GOAT CHEESE QUESADILLAS:

Ingredients:
- Two zucchini sliced
- 1 red bell pepper, sliced
- 1 yellow onion, sliced
- 1 tablespoon olive oil
- Salt and pepper to taste
- 4 large flour tortillas
- 4 oz. crumbled goat cheese
- 1/4 cup chopped fresh cilantro

Instructions:
1. Turn the grill's heat up to medium-high.
2. Add olive oil, salt, and pepper to taste, and toss the thinly sliced zucchini, red bell pepper, and yellow onion.
3. Grill the vegetables for 5 to 7 minutes or until they soften and brown.
4. Arrange the flour tortillas on a table and distribute the grilled vegetables among them.

5. Top the vegetables with goat cheese that has been crumbled and fresh cilantro that has been finely chopped.
6. To make quesadillas, fold the tortillas in half.
7. Grill the quesadillas for 1 to 2 minutes on each side or until the cheese is melted and the tortillas start to sear.
8. Present the goat cheese and grilled vegetable quesadillas hot.

BAKED SALMON WITH BROCCOLI AND CAULIFLOWER GRATIN:

Ingredients:
- 4 salmon fillets
- 1 head of broccoli, chopped
- 1 head cauliflower, chopped
- 2 tablespoons olive oil
- Salt and pepper to taste
- 1/4 cup butter
- 1/4 cup all-purpose flour
- 2 cups milk
- 1/2 teaspoon ground nutmeg
- 1/2 teaspoon garlic powder
- 1/2 cup grated Parmesan cheese

Instructions:
1. Set the oven to 375 degrees.
2. Set aside the salmon fillets in a baking tray.
3. Add salt and pepper to taste, and toss the chopped cauliflower and broccoli with the olive oil.
4. In the baking dish, distribute the broccoli and cauliflower around the salmon fillets.

5. Cook the salmon and veggies in the oven for 15 to 20 minutes or until they are cooked through and soft.
6. Melt the butter in a medium skillet over medium heat while the salmon bakes.
7. Cook for 1-2 minutes after adding the all-purpose flour and whisking until smooth.
8. Until the mixture is smooth, gradually whisk in the milk, nutmeg, garlic powder, salt, and pepper.
9. Cook the sauce for 5 to 7 minutes, stirring often, until it thickens.
10. Once the grated Parmesan cheese has melted, add it.
11. Plate the hot veggies and baked salmon with broccoli and cauliflower gratin.

CHICKEN AND VEGETABLE STIR-FRY WITH BROWN RICE:

Ingredients:

- 1 lb. boneless, skinless chicken breast, cut into bite-sized pieces
- 1 tablespoon cornstarch
- 1 tablespoon soy sauce
- 1 tablespoon sesame oil
- 2 tablespoons olive oil
- 1 red bell pepper, sliced
- 1 green bell pepper, sliced
- 1 onion, sliced
- 2 cloves garlic, minced
- 2 cups cooked brown rice

Instructions:

1. Combine the cornstarch, soy sauce, and sesame oil in a small bowl and whisk until combined.
2. Add the chicken pieces and stir to coat in the basin.
3. Heat the olive oil in a large skillet over medium-high heat.
4. Add the sliced red, green, and onion to the skillet and cook for 3–4 minutes or until the vegetables start softening.
5. Stir in the minced garlic and cook for a few minutes or until fragrant.
6. Add the chicken to the skillet with the cornstarch mixture, and heat for 5 to 7 minutes, or until the chicken is thoroughly cooked and starting to brown.
7. Spoon the hot chicken and vegetable stir-fry over a bed of brown rice prepared.

LENTIL AND VEGETABLE TACOS WITH WHOLE WHEAT TORTILLAS:

Ingredients:
- 1 tablespoon olive oil
- 1 onion, chopped
- 2 cloves garlic, minced
- 1 red bell pepper, chopped
- 1 yellow squash, chopped
- 1 zucchini, chopped
- 1 can (15 oz.) lentils, drained and rinsed
- 1 tablespoon chili powder
- 1 teaspoon ground cumin
- Salt and pepper to taste
- 8 whole wheat tortillas
- 1/4 cup chopped fresh cilantro

- 1 lime, cut into wedges

Instructions:

1. Heat the olive oil in a large skillet over medium-high heat.
2. Include the minced garlic and diced onion in the skillet and cook for 2–3 minutes or until soft.
3. Add the diced yellow squash, zucchini, and red bell pepper to the skillet and cook for 5 to 7 minutes or until slightly softened.
4. Add the lentils rinsed and drained to the skillet and toss in the chili powder, cumin powder, salt, and pepper.
5. Heat the lentil and vegetable mixture for 3 to 4 minutes.
6. Microwave or dry skillet to warm the whole wheat tortillas.
7. Fill the tortillas with the warm lentil and veggie mixture and top with freshly chopped cilantro.
8. Place lime wedges on the side and serve the tacos with lentils and vegetables hot.

SHRIMP AND VEGETABLE CURRY WITH BROWN RICE:

Ingredients:

- 1 lb. shrimp, peeled and deveined
- 1 tablespoon olive oil
- 1 onion, chopped
- 2 cloves garlic, minced
- 1 red bell pepper, chopped
- 1 yellow squash, chopped
- 1 zucchini, chopped
- 1 can (15 oz.) chickpeas, drained and rinsed

- 1 can (14 oz.) coconut milk
- 2 tablespoons curry powder
- Salt and pepper to taste
- 2 cups cooked brown rice

Instructions:

1. Heat the olive oil in a large skillet over medium-high heat.
2. Include the minced garlic and diced onion in the skillet and cook for 2–3 minutes or until soft.
3. Add the diced yellow squash, zucchini, and red bell pepper to the skillet and cook for 5 to 7 minutes or until slightly softened.
4. Stir together the deveined and peeled shrimp, chickpeas that have been rinsed and drained, curry powder, salt, and pepper in the skillet.
5. Stir the shrimp and vegetable combination while adding the coconut milk.
6. Lower the heat to a low setting, cover, and cook the shrimp and vegetable curry for 5 to 7 minutes, or until the shrimp is cooked and the veggies are soft.
7. Spoon the hot shrimp and vegetable curry over a serving of brown rice that has been cooked.

BAKED COD WITH ROASTED RED PEPPER SAUCE AND SAUTÉED SPINACH:

Ingredients:

- 4 cod fillets
- 2 tablespoons olive oil
- Salt and pepper to taste
- 1 jar (12 oz.) roasted red peppers, drained
- 2 cloves garlic, minced
- 1/4 cup grated Parmesan cheese
- 1/4 cup chopped fresh parsley
- 2 tablespoons butter
- 1 lb. fresh spinach leaves

Instructions:

1. Set the oven to 375 degrees.
2. Arrange the fish fillets in a baking tray and drizzle with olive oil. Add salt and pepper to taste.
3. To cook the cod fillets so they flake easily with a fork, bake them in the oven for 15 to 20 minutes.
4. Prepare the roasted red pepper sauce while the fish bakes. In a blender or food processor, combine the drained roasted red peppers, minced garlic, grated Parmesan cheese, and chopped fresh parsley until smooth.
5. Place a large skillet over medium heat and melt the butter.
6. Toss in the fresh spinach leaves and cook for 3 to 4 minutes or until the spinach wilts.
7. Plate the hot baked cod and top it with the sautéed spinach and roasted red pepper sauce.

CHAPTER 7: RECIPES FOR DESSERT

FRESH FRUIT SALAD WITH GREEK YOGURT AND HONEY:

Ingredients:

- 2 cups mixed fresh fruit (such as berries, sliced kiwi, and chopped mango)
- 1/2 cup Greek yogurt
- 1 tablespoon honey
- 1/4 cup chopped nuts (such as almonds, walnuts, or pecans)

Instructions:

1. Place the fresh fruit in a big bowl after washing and preparing it as you like.
2. Combine the Greek yogurt and honey in another bowl.
3. Spread the Greek yogurt and honey mixture over the fresh fruit, then toss everything together gently.
4. Decorate the fruit salad with the chopped nuts.
5. Present the fruit salad right away.

BAKED APPLES WITH CINNAMON AND WALNUTS:

Ingredients:

- Four large apples (such as Honeycrisp or Granny Smith)
- 1/4 cup chopped walnuts
- 1 teaspoon cinnamon
- 1 tablespoon honey
- 2 tablespoons butter

Instructions:

1. Set the oven to 375 degrees.
2. Cut the top off each apple, then scoop out the core and seeds with a spoon or melon baller.
3. Combine the honey, cinnamon, and walnuts in a small bowl.
4. Place a spoonful of the walnut mixture in the apple's core.
5. Place a small piece of butter on top of each apple.
6. After stuffing the apples, place them on a baking tray and bake for 30-35 minutes or until they are delicate and squishy.
7. Depending on preference, top the warm-cooked apples with more chopped walnuts.

CHOCOLATE AVOCADO PUDDING:

Ingredients:

- 2 ripe avocados
- 1/2 cup unsweetened cocoa powder
- 1/2 cup honey
- 1/2 cup almond milk
- 1 teaspoon vanilla extract
- Pinch of salt

Instructions:

1. Halve the avocados and scoop out the pit. Scoop out the flesh and add it to a food processor or blender.
2. Fill the blender or food processor with cocoa powder, honey, almond milk, vanilla extract, and salt.
3. Purée the mixture until it is creamy and smooth.
4. Before serving, divide the chocolate avocado pudding among serving bowls and refrigerate in the fridge for at least an hour.
5. If preferred, top the cooled chocolate avocado pudding with fresh fruit or chopped almonds.

BERRY AND YOGURT PARFAIT WITH GRANOLA:

Ingredients:

- 1 cup plain Greek yogurt
- 1/2 cup mixed fresh berries (such as raspberries, blueberries, and sliced strawberries)
- 1/4 cup granola
- 1 tablespoon honey

Instructions:

1. Combine the Greek yogurt and honey in a small bowl.
2. Spoon some of the yogurt mixtures into a glass or bowl's bottom.
3. Top the yogurt with a layer of fresh berries that have been blended.
4. Cover the berries with a layer of granola.
5. Continue layering the glass or bowl until it is filled.
6. Immediately serve the yogurt and berry parfait.

POACHED PEARS WITH HONEY AND CINNAMON:

Ingredients:

- 4 ripe pears
- 1/4 cup honey
- 1 cinnamon stick
- 1 teaspoon vanilla extract
- 2 cups water

Instructions:

1. Pears can be peeled with the stems still attached.
2. Mix the honey, cinnamon stick, vanilla extract, and water in a big pot.
3. Use medium-high heat to bring the mixture to a boil.
4. Lower the heat to a low setting and stir in the pears.
5. Boil the pears for 20 to 25 minutes or until they are soft and pierce readily with a fork.
6. Please take the pears from the pot and give them a minute to cool.
7. Drizzle some of the poaching liquid over the warm poached pears before serving.

GRILLED PINEAPPLE WITH GREEK YOGURT AND HONEY:

Ingredients:

- 1 pineapple, peeled and cored
- 1/2 cup plain Greek yogurt
- 2 tablespoons honey
- 1/4 cup chopped nuts (such as almonds or pecans)

Instructions:

1. Set a grill or grill pan to medium-high heat in step 1.
2. The pineapple should be cut into wedges.
3. Grill the pineapple wedges on each side for two to three minutes or until they begin to sear and caramelize.
4. Combine the Greek yogurt and honey in a small bowl.
5. Top the hot, grilled pineapple with a dollop of the yogurt mixture, some chopped almonds, and a sprinkle of cinnamon.

MIXED BERRY CRUMBLE WITH ALMOND FLOUR TOPPING:

Ingredients:

- 4 cups mixed fresh or frozen berries (such as raspberries, blueberries, and blackberries)
- 1/4 cup honey
- 1/4 cup almond flour
- 1/4 cup old-fashioned oats
- 1/4 cup chopped nuts (such as almonds or pecans)
- 2 tablespoons butter, melted
- Pinch of salt

Instructions:

1. Set the oven to 375 degrees.
2. Combine the berries and honey in a sizable bowl.
3. Fill the baking dish with the fruit mixture.
4. Combine the almond flour, oats, chopped almonds, melted butter, and salt in another bowl until a crumbly mixture forms.
5. Evenly cover the berry mixture with the crumble mixture.
6. Bake the mixed berry crumble in the oven for 25 to 30 minutes or until the top is golden and the filling bubbles.
7. If desired, top the warm mixed berry crumble with a dollop of whipped cream or a scoop of vanilla ice cream.

CHIA SEED PUDDING WITH COCONUT MILK AND MANGO:

Ingredients:

- 1/2 cup chia seeds
- 2 cups coconut milk
- 1 tablespoon honey
- 1 teaspoon vanilla extract
- 1 mango, peeled and chopped

Instructions:

1. Combine the chia seeds, coconut milk, honey, and vanilla essence in a big bowl.
2. Allow the mixture to stand for at least 10 minutes or until the chia seeds have thickened and absorbed some liquid.
3. Add the chopped mango and stir.
4. Before serving, divide the chia seed pudding among serving bowls and refrigerate in the fridge for at least an hour.
5. You can serve the cooled chia seed pudding with more chopped mango or shredded coconut on top.

PEACH AND BLUEBERRY CRISP WITH OATMEAL TOPPING:

Ingredients:

- 4 ripe peaches, peeled and sliced
- 2 cups fresh blueberries
- 1/4 cup honey
- 1 tablespoon cornstarch
- 1/4 cup old-fashioned oats
- 1/4 cup almond flour
- 1/4 cup chopped nuts (such as almonds or pecans)
- 2 tablespoons butter, melted
- Pinch of salt

Instructions:

1. Set the oven to 375 degrees.
2. Combine the blueberries, honey, peach slices, and cornstarch in a bowl.
3. Fill the baking dish with the fruit mixture.
4. Combine the oats, almond flour, chopped almonds, melted butter, and salt in another bowl until a crumbly mixture forms.
5. Cover the fruit mixture with a uniform layer of the oatmeal topping.
6. Bake the peach and blueberry crisp for 25 to 30 minutes, until the fruit mixture bubbles and the top is golden brown.
7. To serve the peach and blueberry crisp, keep it warm and top it with whipped cream or a scoop of vanilla ice cream, as desired.

LEMON POPPY SEED MUFFINS WITH ALMOND FLOUR:

Ingredients:

- 2 cups almond flour
- 1/4 cup coconut flour
- 1/2 teaspoon baking soda
- 1/4 teaspoon salt
- 3 eggs
- 1/4 cup honey
- 1/4 cup melted coconut oil
- 2 tablespoons lemon zest
- 1 tablespoon poppy seeds
- 1 tablespoon lemon juice

Instructions:

1. Set the oven's temperature to 350°F.
2. Combine the salt, baking soda, almond flour, and coconut flour in a sizable basin.
3. Combine the eggs, honey, melted coconut oil, lemon zest, poppy seeds, and lemon juice in another bowl.
4. Combine the dry ingredients with the liquid components after adding them.
5. Use muffin liners to line the tin and distribute the batter evenly among the cups.
6. Bake the lemon poppy seed muffins in the oven for 20 to 25 minutes or until a toothpick inserted in the center comes out clean.
7. After the muffins have cooled in the pan for five minutes, move them to a wire rack to finish cooling.

DARK CHOCOLATE AND ALMOND BUTTER BITES:

Ingredients:
- 1/2 cup almond butter
- 1/4 cup honey
- 1/4 cup coconut flour
- 1/4 cup dark chocolate chips
- 1/4 cup chopped nuts (such as almonds or pecans)

Instructions:
1. Combine the coconut flour, honey, and almond butter in a big bowl until a thick dough forms.
2. Combine the chopped nuts and dark chocolate chips.
3. Form the dough into small balls for your mouth.
4. At least 30 minutes before serving, put the bite-sized pieces of dark chocolate and almond butter in the refrigerator.
5. Present the bites cold.

MIXED BERRY SMOOTHIE WITH ALMOND MILK AND CHIA SEEDS:

Ingredients:
- 1 cup mixed fresh or frozen berries (such as raspberries, blueberries, and blackberries)
- 1 cup unsweetened almond milk
- 1 tablespoon chia seeds
- 1 tablespoon honey
- 1 teaspoon vanilla extract

Instructions:
1. Mash up the mixed berries with the almond milk, chia seeds, honey, and vanilla essence in a blender.
2. Purée the mixture until it is creamy and smooth.
3. Pour the smoothie of mixed berries into a glass and serve right away.

BLUEBERRY AND GREEK YOGURT POPSICLES:

Ingredients:
- 2 cups plain Greek yogurt
- 1 cup fresh or frozen blueberries
- 2 tablespoons honey
- 1 teaspoon vanilla extract

Instructions:
1. Combine Greek yogurt, blueberries, honey, and vanilla extract in a blender.
2. Purée the mixture until it is creamy and smooth.
3. Spoon the mixture into popsicle molds and freeze for at least 4 hours to achieve solid popsicles.

4. To release the popsicles from the molds, briefly submerge them in warm water. Then, remove the popsicles and serve.

APPLE CINNAMON OATMEAL COOKIES WITH COCONUT FLOUR:

Ingredients:
- 1 1/2 cups coconut flour
- 1/2 cup old-fashioned oats
- 1/2 cup unsweetened applesauce
- 1/4 cup honey
- 1/4 cup melted coconut oil
- 1 egg
- 1 teaspoon vanilla extract
- 1 teaspoon ground cinnamon
- 1/2 teaspoon baking soda
- Pinch of salt

Instructions:
1. Set the oven's temperature to 350°F.
2. Combine coconut flour, oats, cinnamon powder, baking soda, and salt in a sizable basin.
3. Combine the applesauce, honey, melted coconut oil, egg, and vanilla extract in another bowl.
4. Combine the dry ingredients and liquid components until a dough forms.
5. Drop tablespoon-sized portions of the dough onto a baking sheet coated with parchment paper.
6. Use a fork to flatten each biscuit.
7. Bake the oatmeal cookies with apple cinnamon for 12 to 15 minutes or until golden brown and firm.

8. After the cookies have cooled on the baking sheet for five minutes, move them to a wire rack to finish cooling.

STRAWBERRY AND AVOCADO SMOOTHIE BOWL:

Ingredients:
- 1 ripe avocado, peeled and pitted
- 1 cup frozen strawberries
- 1/2 cup unsweetened almond milk
- 1 tablespoon honey
- 1 tablespoon chia seeds

Instructions:
1. Combine the avocado, thawed strawberries, almond milk, honey, and chia seeds in a blender.
2. Purée the mixture until it is creamy and smooth.
3. Spoon the strawberry and avocado smoothie into a bowl and garnish with your preferred ingredients, such as granola, shredded coconut, or thinly sliced fresh fruit.

CHOCOLATE AND PEANUT BUTTER PROTEIN BALLS:

Ingredients:

- 1 cup rolled oats
- 1/2 cup natural peanut butter
- 1/3 cup honey
- 1/4 cup chocolate protein powder
- 1/4 cup dark chocolate chips

Instructions:

1. Combine the rolled oats, peanut butter, honey, and chocolate protein powder in a big bowl.
2. Add the dark chocolate chips by folding them.
3. Make bite-sized balls out of the mixture.
4. Before serving, place the chocolate and peanut butter protein balls in the refrigerator for at least 30 minutes.
5. Present the frozen balls.

MANGO AND COCONUT CHIA SEED PUDDING:

Ingredients:

- 1 cup unsweetened coconut milk
- 1/4 cup chia seeds
- 1 tablespoon honey
- 1/2 teaspoon vanilla extract
- 1 ripe mango, peeled and diced

Instructions:

1. Combine coconut milk, chia seeds, honey, and vanilla essence in a medium bowl.

2. Ten minutes later, stir the mixture once or twice.
3. Add the diced mango and stir.
4. Refrigerate the mango and coconut chia seed pudding for at least two hours or overnight by covering the bowl with plastic wrap.
5. Present the pudding cold.

ROASTED PEARS WITH BALSAMIC GLAZE AND WALNUTS:

Ingredients:
- 4 ripe pears, halved and cored
- 1/4 cup balsamic vinegar
- 2 tablespoons honey
- 1/2 teaspoon ground cinnamon
- 1/4 cup chopped walnuts

Instructions:
1. Set the oven to 375 degrees.
2. Arrange the pear halves on a parchment-lined baking pan.
3. Combine the balsamic vinegar, honey, and ground cinnamon in a small bowl.
4. Apply the mixture to the pears by brushing.
5. Bake the pears for 20 to 25 minutes or until soft and browned.
6. Top the roasted pears with the chopped walnuts.
7. Arrange the heated walnuts and balsamic glaze on top of the roasted pears.

VEGAN BANANA BREAD WITH ALMOND FLOUR AND COCONUT OIL:

Ingredients:

- 3 ripe bananas, mashed
- 1/3 cup coconut oil, melted
- 1/3 cup maple syrup
- 1 teaspoon vanilla extract
- 2 cups almond flour
- 1 teaspoon baking powder
- 1/2 teaspoon baking soda
- 1/2 teaspoon salt

Instructions:

1. Set the oven's temperature to 350°F.
2. Combine the mashed bananas, melted coconut oil, maple syrup, and vanilla extract
3. in a sizable bowl.
4. Combine the salt, baking soda, baking powder, and almond flour in another bowl.
5. Combine the dry and wet components thoroughly after adding the dry ingredients.
6. Spoon the batter into a loaf pan that has been oiled.
7. Cook the vegan banana bread in the oven for 50 to 60 minutes or until a toothpick inserted into the center comes clean.
8. Before removing and slicing the banana bread, allow it to cool in the pan for 10 minutes.

ORANGE AND ALMOND FLOUR CAKE WITH HONEY GLAZE:

Ingredients:

- 2 cups almond flour
- 1/2 cup honey
- 1/4 cup coconut oil, melted
- 4 eggs
- 1/4 cup orange juice
- 2 tablespoons orange zest
- 1 teaspoon baking soda
- Pinch of salt

For the glaze:

- 1/4 cup honey
- 1 tablespoon orange juice

Instructions:

1. Set the oven's temperature to 350°F.
2. Combine the almond flour, honey, melted coconut oil, eggs, orange juice, orange zest, baking soda, and salt in a sizable basin.
3. Spoon the batter onto a cake pan that has been buttered.
4. Bake the cake made with almond and orange flour for 25 to 30 minutes or until a toothpick inserted in the center comes out clean.
5. After the cake has cooled in the pan for ten minutes, remove it and set it on a wire rack to finish cooling.
6. Combine the honey and orange juice in a separate bowl to make the glaze.
7. Pour the honey glaze over the chilled cake made with orange and almond flour.

COCONUT AND ALMOND FLOUR COOKIES WITH DARK CHOCOLATE CHIPS:

Ingredients:

- 2 cups almond flour
- 1/2 cup shredded coconut
- 1/2 cup dark chocolate chips
- 1/4 cup coconut oil, melted
- 1/4 cup maple syrup
- 1 egg
- 1/2 teaspoon baking soda
- Pinch of salt

Instructions:

1. Set the oven's temperature to 350°F.
2. Combine the almond flour, coconut shreds, dark chocolate chips, melted coconut oil, maple syrup, egg, baking soda, and salt in a sizable basin.
3. Drop tablespoon-sized portions of the dough onto a baking sheet coated with parchment paper.
4. Use a fork to flatten each biscuit.
5. Bake the cookies made with almond and coconut flour for 12 to 15 minutes or until golden brown and firm.
6. After the cookies have cooled on the baking sheet for five minutes, move them to a wire rack to finish cooling.

CHOCOLATE AND CHERRY CHIA SEED PUDDING:

Ingredients:

- 1 cup unsweetened almond milk
- 1/4 cup chia seeds
- 2 tablespoons maple syrup
- 1 tablespoon unsweetened cocoa powder
- 1/4 teaspoon vanilla extract
- 1/4 cup fresh cherries, pitted and chopped

Instructions:

1. In a medium bowl, stir the almond milk, chia seeds, maple syrup, chocolate powder, and vanilla extract.
2. After the mixture has sat for 5 minutes, whisk it once more to incorporate the chia seeds.
3. Put the bowl in the refrigerator overnight or for at least 4 hours.
4. Add the cherry halves just before serving, and enjoy.

PEANUT BUTTER AND JELLY SMOOTHIE WITH ALMOND MILK AND CHIA SEEDS:

Ingredients:

- 1 cup unsweetened almond milk
- 1 banana, sliced and frozen
- 1/4 cup frozen mixed berries
- 2 tablespoons peanut butter
- 1 tablespoon chia seeds
- 1 teaspoon honey

Instructions:

1. Place all ingredients in a blender and process until they are creamy and smooth.
2. Transfer the smoothie to a glass, then quickly sip on it.

CARROT AND WALNUT MUFFINS WITH COCONUT FLOUR:

Ingredients:
- 1 cup coconut flour
- 1 teaspoon baking soda
- 1/2 teaspoon ground cinnamon
- 1/4 teaspoon ground ginger
- Pinch of salt
- 4 eggs
- 1/2 cup unsweetened applesauce
- 1/4 cup honey
- 1 teaspoon vanilla extract
- 2 cups grated carrots
- 1/2 cup chopped walnuts

Instructions:
1. Set the oven's temperature to 350°F.
2. Combine the salt, baking soda, cinnamon, ginger, and coconut flour in a sizable basin.
3. Combine the eggs, applesauce, honey, and vanilla extract in another bowl.
4. Combine the dry ingredients with the liquid components after adding them.
5. Combine the chopped walnuts and grated carrots.
6. Use coconut oil or cooking spray to grease a muffin pan.
7. Distribute the batter equally among the muffin tins.

8. Bake the muffins with the walnuts and carrots for 20 to 25 minutes or until a toothpick inserted into the center comes out clean.
9. After the muffins have cooled in the pan for five minutes, move them to a wire rack to finish cooling.

GREEK YOGURT AND BERRY ICE CREAM WITH HONEY:

Ingredients:

- 2 cups frozen mixed berries
- 1 cup plain Greek yogurt
- 2 tablespoons honey
- 1/2 teaspoon vanilla extract

Instructions:

1. Fill a blender or food processor with the frozen berries, Greek yogurt, honey, and vanilla extract.
2. Purée the mixture until it is creamy and smooth.
3. Transfer the Greek yogurt and berry ice cream to a freezer-safe container, freeze it for later use, or serve it immediately.

VANILLA AND ALMOND FLOUR CUPCAKES WITH GREEK YOGURT FROSTING:

Ingredients:

For the cupcakes:

- 2 cups almond flour
- 1/2 teaspoon baking soda
- 1/4 teaspoon salt
- 3 eggs
- 1/4 cup coconut oil, melted
- 1/4 cup honey
- 1 teaspoon vanilla extract

For the frosting:

- 1 cup plain Greek yogurt
- 2 tablespoons honey
- 1/4 teaspoon vanilla extract

Instructions:

For the cupcakes:

1. Set the oven's temperature to 350°F.
2. Combine the salt, baking soda, and almond flour in a big bowl.
3. Combine the eggs, melted coconut oil, honey, and vanilla extract in another bowl.
4. Combine the dry ingredients with the liquid components after adding them.
5. Distribute the batter equally among the 12 muffin tins.
6. Cook the cupcakes in the oven for 20 to 25 minutes or until a toothpick inserted into the center comes clean.

7. After the cupcakes have cooled in the pan for five minutes, move them to a wire rack to finish cooling.

For the frosting:

1. In a small bowl, combine the Greek yogurt, honey, and vanilla essence and whisk until combined.
2. After the cupcakes have cooled, top each one with the Greek yogurt frosting.

GRILLED PEACHES WITH HONEY AND CINNAMON:

Ingredients:
- 4 ripe peaches, halved and pitted
- 2 tablespoons honey
- 1/2 teaspoon ground cinnamon
- Vanilla Greek yogurt for serving

Instructions:
1. Turn on the medium heat and prepare a grill or grill pan.
2. Sprinkle cinnamon and honey on the peach halves that have been chopped.
3. Grill the peaches for 2 to 3 minutes or until they have grill marks and are just beginning to soften.
4. After grilling the peaches for 1 to 2 more minutes, flip them over.
5. Place a dollop of vanilla Greek yogurt on the grilled peaches before serving.

APPLE AND ALMOND BUTTER CRUMBLE WITH OATMEAL TOPPING:

Ingredients:

For the filling:

- 4 medium apples, peeled and sliced
- 1/4 cup almond butter
- 2 tablespoons honey
- 1 teaspoon cinnamon
- 1/4 teaspoon nutmeg

For the topping:

- 1 cup rolled oats
- 1/4 cup almond flour
- 1/4 cup chopped almonds
- 2 tablespoons honey
- 2 tablespoons coconut oil, melted
- 1 teaspoon cinnamon
- 1/4 teaspoon salt

Instructions:

1. Set the oven to 375 degrees.
2. Combine the apple slices, almond butter, honey, cinnamon, and nutmeg in a sizable bowl.
3. Spread the apple mixture evenly across a 9-inch baking dish.
4. Combine the rolled oats, almond flour, chopped almonds, honey, melted coconut oil, cinnamon, and salt in another bowl.
5. Top the apple mixture with the oatmeal mixture.

6. Bake the crumbled apple and almond butter for 30-35 minutes or until the topping is golden and the apples are soft.
7. Before serving, let the crumble cool for 5 to 10 minutes.

CHOCOLATE AND RASPBERRY SMOOTHIE BOWL:

Ingredients:

- 1 banana, frozen
- 1 cup frozen raspberries
- 1/2 cup unsweetened almond milk
- 1 tablespoon almond butter
- 1 tablespoon cocoa powder
- 1/4 teaspoon vanilla extract
- Fresh raspberries for topping
- Sliced almonds for topping

Instructions:

1. Combine the frozen banana, raspberries, almond milk, almond butter, chocolate powder, and vanilla extract in a blender or food processor.
2. Purée the mixture until it is creamy and smooth.
3. Pour the smoothie into a serving bowl.
4. Before serving, garnish the smoothie with fresh raspberries and sliced almonds.

COCONUT AND ALMOND FLOUR PANCAKES WITH FRESH BERRIES:

Ingredients:

- 1/2 cup almond flour
- 1/4 cup coconut flour
- 1/4 teaspoon baking soda
- 1/4 teaspoon salt
- 4 eggs
- 1/4 cup unsweetened almond milk
- 1/4 cup coconut oil, melted
- 1 tablespoon honey
- Fresh berries for serving
- Greek yogurt for serving

Instructions:

1. Combine the salt, baking soda, coconut, and almond flour in a big basin.
2. Combine the eggs, almond milk, melted coconut oil, and honey in another bowl.
3. Combine the dry ingredients with the wet components after adding them.
4. Melt extra coconut oil or frying spray in a large skillet or griddle over medium heat.
5. Scoop the pancake batter onto the skillet or griddle using a 1/4 cup measure.
6. Cook the pancakes for 2-3 minutes on each side or until golden brown and thoroughly cooked.
7. Arrange a dollop of Greek yogurt on top of each pancake and top with fresh berries.

CHAPTER 8: RECIPES FOR SMACKS

APPLE SLICES WITH ALMOND BUTTER:

Ingredients:

- 1 apple
- 2 tablespoons almond butter
- Cinnamon (optional)

Instructions:

1. Remove the apple's core before cutting it into pieces.
2. Spread each piece with almond butter.
3. Optionally, top with cinnamon.
4. Dish out and savor!

CARROT STICKS WITH HUMMUS:

Ingredients:
- 2 carrots
- 1/4 cup hummus

Instructions:
1. Peel and cut the carrots into sticks.
2. Serve with hummus for dipping.
3. Enjoy!

HARD-BOILED EGGS:

Ingredients:
- 2 eggs
- Water

Instructions:
1. Fill a pot with cold water and add the eggs to it.
2. Heat the water to a rolling boil.
3. After the water boils, remove the pot and put a lid on it.
4. Allow the eggs to rest in the boiling water for 10 to 12 minutes.
5. After rinsing the eggs in cold water, drain the hot water.
6. After peeling, eat the eggs as a snack.

APPLE SLICES WITH ALMOND BUTTER:

Ingredients:
- One apple
- 2 tablespoons almond butter
- Cinnamon (optional)

Instructions:
1. Remove the apple's core before cutting it into pieces.
2. Spread each piece with almond butter.
3. Optionally, top with cinnamon.
4. Dish out and savor!

CARROT STICKS WITH HUMMUS:

Ingredients:
- 2 carrots
- 1/4 cup hummus

Instructions:
1. Peel the carrots and chop them into sticks.
2. Offer hummus for dipping alongside.
3. Enjoy!

HARD-BOILED EGGS:

Ingredients:
- Two eggs
- Water

Instructions:
1. Fill a pot with cold water and add the eggs to it.
2. Heat the water to a rolling boil.

3. After the water boils, remove the pot and put a lid on it.
4. Allow the eggs to rest in the boiling water for 10 to 12 minutes.
5. After rinsing the eggs in cold water, drain the hot water.
6. After peeling, eat the eggs as a snack.

GREEK YOGURT WITH MIXED BERRIES:

Ingredients:

- 1/2 cup Greek yogurt
- 1/2 cup mixed berries (such as blueberries, strawberries, and raspberries)
- 1 tablespoon honey (optional)

Instructions:

1. Pour a bowl with the Greek yogurt.
2. Add various berries on top.
3. If desired, drizzle with honey.
4. Dish out and savor!

SLICED CUCUMBER WITH TZATZIKI SAUCE:

Ingredients:

- 1 cucumber
- 1/4 cup tzatziki sauce

Instructions:

1. After washing, slice the cucumber into rounds.
2. Offer tzatziki sauce for dipping with the dish.
3. Enjoy!

TRAIL MIX WITH NUTS AND DRIED FRUIT:

Ingredients:

- 1/2 cup mixed nuts (such as almonds, cashews, and walnuts)
- 1/4 cup dried fruit (such as raisins, cranberries, and apricots)
- 1/4 cup dark chocolate chips (optional)

Instructions:

1. In a bowl, combine the nuts, dried fruit, and dark chocolate chips (if using).
2. Place the trail mix in an airtight container.
3. Enjoy it as a portable snack!

EDAMAME:

Ingredients:

- 1 cup edamame (frozen or fresh)
- Salt

Instructions:

1. If using frozen edamame, prepare as directed on the package. Boil fresh edamame for 5 to 10 minutes until they are tender.
2. Drain the edamame, then salt them.
3. Dish out and savor!

ROASTED CHICKPEAS:

Ingredients:

- 1 can chickpeas, drained and rinsed
- 1 tablespoon olive oil
- 1 teaspoon ground cumin
- 1/2 teaspoon paprika

- Salt and pepper

Instructions:
1. Set the oven's temperature to 400°F (200°C).
2. Using a paper towel, pat the chickpeas dry.
3. In a bowl, combine the chickpeas with the olive oil, cumin, paprika, salt, and pepper.
4. Arrange the chickpeas on a baking sheet in a single layer.
5. Roast until crispy for 25 to 30 minutes, tossing halfway through.
6. Dish out and savor!

DARK CHOCOLATE SQUARES:

Ingredients:
- 1 bar (3.5 ounces) of dark chocolate (70% or higher cocoa content)

Instructions:
1. Cut the chocolate bar into modest squares.
2. In a double boiler or microwave, melt the chocolate while stirring constantly.
3. Spoon the melted chocolate onto parchment paper or a silicone mold.
4. Place the chocolate in the fridge or at room temperature to cool and solidify.
5. Slicing the chocolate into small pieces.
6. Savour several squares as a tasty treat!

CHERRY TOMATOES WITH FETA CHEESE:

Ingredients:
- 1 cup cherry tomatoes
- 1/4 cup crumbled feta cheese
- 1 tablespoon chopped fresh basil
- Salt and pepper

Instructions:
1. Cut the cherry tomatoes in half after washing them.
2. Combine the tomatoes, feta cheese, and fresh basil in a bowl.
3. Add some salt and pepper.
4. Dish out and savor!

COTTAGE CHEESE WITH PINEAPPLE CHUNKS:

Ingredients:
- 1/2 cup cottage cheese
- 1/2 cup pineapple chunks

Instructions:
1. Place a bowl with the cottage cheese in it.
2. Add pineapple slices on top.
3. Dish out and savor!

AVOCADO AND TOMATO SALSA WITH WHOLE GRAIN CHIPS:

Ingredients:

- 1 avocado, diced
- 1 tomato, diced
- 1/4 red onion, diced
- 1/4 cup chopped fresh cilantro
- 1 tablespoon lime juice
- Salt and pepper
- Whole grain tortilla chips

Instructions:

1. Combine the lime juice, cilantro, tomato, red onion, and avocado in a bowl.
2. Add salt and pepper to taste.
3. To go with whole-grain tortilla chips, serve the salsa.
4. Enjoy!

POPCORN WITH NUTRITIONAL YEAST:

Ingredients:

- 1/2 cup popcorn kernels
- 2 tablespoons nutritional yeast
- 1 tablespoon olive oil
- Salt and pepper

Instructions:

1. Prepare the popcorn kernels following the directions on the package.
2. Combine the popcorn, nutritional yeast, olive oil, salt, and pepper in a bowl.

3. Stir to coat thoroughly.
4. Dish out and savor!

TURKEY AND CHEESE ROLL-UPS:

Ingredients:
- 4 slices deli turkey
- 4 slices cheddar cheese
- 1/4 cup baby spinach leaves

Instructions:
1. On a chopping board, arrange the turkey slices flatly.
2. Top each slice of turkey with a piece of cheese and a few spinach leaves.
3. Tightly enclose the cheese and spinach with the turkey slices.
4. Use a toothpick to hold each roll-up closed.
5. Present and savor!

ENERGY BALLS WITH NUTS AND DRIED FRUIT:

Ingredients:
- 1 cup mixed nuts (such as almonds, cashews, and walnuts)
- 1/2 cup dried fruit (such as raisins, dates, and apricots)
- 1/4 cup almond butter
- 1 tablespoon honey
- 1/4 teaspoon cinnamon
- Pinch of salt

Instructions:
1. In a food processor, pulse the mixed nuts and dried fruit until they are finely chopped.

2. Include honey, cinnamon, almond butter, and salt. Pulse to combine the ingredients and make them slightly sticky.
3. Form the mixture into little balls with your hands.
4. Set the energy balls in the refrigerator for at least 30 minutes on a plate or in an airtight container.
5. Present and savor!

BAKED SWEET POTATO FRIES:

Ingredients:
- 2 medium sweet potatoes, peeled and cut into fries
- 1 tablespoon olive oil
- 1/2 teaspoon paprika
- 1/4 teaspoon garlic powder
- Salt and pepper

Instructions:
1. Set the oven's temperature to 400 °F (200 °C).
2. Combine the olive oil, paprika, garlic powder, salt, and pepper in a bowl with the sweet potato fries.
3. Toss to coat evenly.
4. Arrange the fries on a baking sheet in a single layer.
5. Bake the fries for 20 to 25 minutes or until golden and crispy.
6. Present and savor!

GRILLED ZUCCHINI WITH PARMESAN CHEESE:

Ingredients:
- 2 medium zucchini, sliced lengthwise into 1/4-inch thick strips
- 1 tablespoon olive oil
- Salt and pepper

- 1/4 cup grated Parmesan cheese

Instructions:

1. Turn the grill's heat up to medium-high.
2. Combine the zucchini strips in a bowl with olive oil, salt, and pepper.
3. Stir to coat thoroughly.
4. Grill the zucchini strips for 3–4 minutes on each side or until they are soft and just starting to brown.
5. Take the zucchini from the grill and top with Parmesan cheese shavings.
6. Dish out and savor!

ANTS ON A LOG (CELERY WITH PEANUT BUTTER AND RAISINS):

Ingredients:
- 4 celery stalks, cut into 3-inch pieces
- 1/4 cup peanut butter
- 1/4 cup raisins

Instructions:
1. Fill the celery slices with peanut butter.
2. Add raisins on top.
3. Dish out and savor!

ROASTED ALMONDS WITH SEA SALT:

Ingredients:
- 1 cup raw almonds
- 1 tablespoon olive oil
- 1/2 teaspoon sea salt

Instructions:
1. Set the oven to 180°C or 350°F.
2. Combine the almonds, sea salt, and olive oil in a bowl.
3. Stir to coat thoroughly.
4. Arrange the almonds on a baking sheet in a single layer.
5. Bake the almonds for 10 to 15 minutes or until they are aromatic and light yellow.
6. Take the food out of the oven and let it cool.
7. Plate and savor!

TUNA SALAD WITH WHOLE GRAIN CRACKERS:

Ingredients:

- 1 can of tuna in water, drained
- 1 tablespoon mayonnaise
- 1 tablespoon plain Greek yogurt
- 1/4 cup chopped celery
- Salt and pepper to taste
- Whole grain crackers for serving

Instructions:

1. Combine the tuna, mayonnaise, Greek yogurt, celery, salt, and pepper in a bowl.
2. Combine by tossing.
3. Pass whole-grain crackers alongside.
4. Enjoy!

HOMEMADE KALE CHIPS:

Ingredients:

- 1 bunch of kale, washed and dried
- 1 tablespoon olive oil
- 1/2 teaspoon garlic powder
- Salt and pepper to taste

Instructions:

1. Set the oven to 180°C or 350°F.
2. Cut the kale leaves into bite-sized pieces after removing the stems.
3. Combine the chopped kale with the olive oil, garlic powder, salt, and pepper in a bowl.
4. Toss to coat evenly.
5. Arrange the kale pieces on a baking sheet in a single layer.

6. Bake the kale chips for 10-15 minutes or until they are crisp and pale brown.
7. Dispatch from the oven, then allow to cool.
8. Dish out and savor!

SLICED BELL PEPPER WITH GUACAMOLE:

Ingredients:
- 1 bell pepper, sliced
- 1 ripe avocado, peeled and pitted
- 1 tablespoon lime juice
- 1/4 teaspoon salt
- 1/4 teaspoon garlic powder
- Pinch of cumin
- Pinch of cayenne pepper

Instructions:
1. Mash the avocado until smooth in a bowl with the lime juice, salt, cumin, garlic powder, and cayenne pepper.
2. Present the guacamole with the cut bell pepper for dipping.
3. Enjoy!

APPLE SLICES WITH CINNAMON AND HONEY:

Ingredients:
- 1 apple, sliced
- 1/2 teaspoon cinnamon
- 1 teaspoon honey

Instructions:
1. Combine the cinnamon and honey in a small bowl.
2. Overlay the apple slices with the mixture.

3. Dish out and savor!

SMOKED SALMON WITH CUCUMBER SLICES:

Ingredients:
- 2 ounces smoked salmon, thinly sliced
- 1/2 cucumber, sliced

Instructions:
1. Place the cucumber slices and smoked salmon on a platter.
2. Dish out and savor!

BANANA AND ALMOND BUTTER BITES:

Ingredients:
- 1 banana, sliced
- 2 tablespoons almond butter
- 1 tablespoon honey
- Pinch of cinnamon

Instructions:
1. Cover each slice of banana with a thin layer of almond butter.
2. Pour honey over the almond butter.
3. Add cinnamon to the bits' tops.
4. Dish out and savor!

GREEK YOGURT WITH HONEY AND GRANOLA:

Ingredients:
- 1/2 cup Greek yogurt
- 1 teaspoon honey

- 1/4 cup granola

Instructions:
1. Greek yogurt and honey should be thoroughly blended in a bowl.
2. Scatter granola over the yogurt concoction.
3. Dish out and savor!

QUINOA SALAD WITH VEGETABLES:

Ingredients:
- 1 cup cooked quinoa
- 1/2 cup cherry tomatoes, halved
- 1/2 cup cucumber, diced
- 1/2 cup red onion, diced
- 1/4 cup fresh parsley, chopped
- 2 tablespoons olive oil
- 1 tablespoon lemon juice
- Salt and pepper to taste

Instructions:
1. Mix the cooked quinoa, cherry tomatoes, cucumber, red onion, and parsley in a big bowl.
2. Combine the olive oil, lemon juice, salt, and pepper in a small bowl.
3. Drizzle the quinoa salad with the dressing and toss to mix.
4. Dish out and savor!

BAKED KALE CHIPS WITH GARLIC AND PARMESAN:

Ingredients:
- 1 bunch of kale, washed and dried
- 2 tablespoons olive oil
- 2 cloves garlic, minced
- 1/4 cup Parmesan cheese, grated
- Salt and pepper to taste

Instructions:
1. Set the oven's temperature to 350°F.
2. Cut the kale leaves into bite-sized pieces and remove the stems.
3. In a big bowl, combine the kale with the olive oil, garlic, Parmesan cheese, salt, and pepper.
4. On a baking sheet, spread the kale out in a single layer.
5. Bake the kale for 10 to 15 minutes or until it is crispy and lightly golden.
6. Take the dish out of the oven, then give it some time to cool.
7. Plate and savor!

WATERMELON CUBES WITH FETA CHEESE:

Ingredients:
- 2 cups watermelon, cubed
- 1/2 cup feta cheese, crumbled
- 2 tablespoons fresh mint leaves, chopped

Instructions:
1. Mix the watermelon, feta cheese, and mint leaves in a bowl.

2. Gently blend by tossing.
3. Dish out and savor!

HUMMUS AND VEGETABLE WRAPS:

Ingredients:
- 4 whole wheat tortillas
- 1/2 cup hummus
- 1/2 cup cherry tomatoes, halved
- 1/2 cup cucumber, sliced
- 1/4 cup red onion, sliced
- 1/4 cup fresh parsley, chopped

Instructions:
1. Arrange the tortillas on a level surface.
2. Spread each tortilla with 2 teaspoons of hummus.
3. Add cherry tomatoes, cucumber, red onion, and parsley to the top of each tortilla.
4. After each tortilla has adequately been rolled, cut it in half.
5. Present and savor!

CHAPTER 9: 28-DAYS MEAL PLAN

FIRST WEEK

Day 1
- Greek yogurt parfait for breakfast with mixed berries and almonds
- Snack: Cucumber slices with tzatziki.
- Grilled chicken salad with vegetables and mixed greens for lunch.
- Apple slices with almond butter as a snack.
- Roasted veggies and salmon over a grill for dinner.

Day 2
- Eggs scrambled with vegetables and whole-wheat bread for breakfast. Carrot sticks with hummus for a snack.
- Lentil soup for lunch with carrots and celery
- Snack: Salt-and-pepper roasted almonds
- Turkey and vegetable chili for dinner

Day 3
- Whole grain oats for breakfast with berries and nuts. Cottage cheese with pineapple chunks for a snack.
- Quinoa salad and grilled shrimp skewers for lunch.
- Snack: Trail mix with dried fruit and almonds.
- Brown rice and grilled tofu kebabs for dinner.

Day 4
- Breakfast: omelet with spinach and feta and whole-grain bread. Snack: edamame
- A side salad and a turkey burger on a whole-wheat bun for lunch.

- Snack: Feta cheese and cherry tomatoes.
- Roasted veggies and chicken in the oven for dinner

Day 5

- Sweet potato hash with eggs for breakfast
- Roasted chickpeas as a snack.
- Brown rice and vegetable curry for lunch.
- Snack: Roll-ups with turkey and cheese
- Cauliflower rice and grilled chicken and vegetables for dinner

Day 6

- Berry-chia seed pudding for breakfast.
- Snack: Squares of dark chocolate
- Fish and boiled vegetables for lunch.
- Food: homemade kale chips.
- Baked sweet potato with berries and Greek yogurt for dinner

Day 7

- Blueberry protein waffles for breakfast
- Snack: Guacamole and sliced bell pepper.
- A chickpea salad with tomatoes and cucumbers for lunch
- Snack: Nutritional yeast-topped popcorn
- Vegetable and lentil stew with brown rice for supper.

SECOND WEEK

Day 1:
1. For breakfast, serve Greek yogurt with a variety of fruit and walnuts.
2. Snack: Hummus and sliced cucumber.
3. A salad with grilled chicken, mixed greens, cherry tomatoes, and avocado for lunch
4. Snack: Almond butter-topped carrot sticks
5. For supper, prepare broiled fish with roasted asparagus and sweet potato wedges.

Day 2:
- Breakfast: an omelet with feta and vegetables on whole-wheat toast. Snack: apple slices with almond butter.
- Lentil soup for lunch with carrots and celery
- Roasted chickpeas as a snack
- Brown rice and grilled tofu kebabs for dinner.

Day 3:
- *Whole grain oats with strawberries and finely chopped almonds for breakfast*
- *Greek yogurt with honey and granola for a snack.*
- *Whole wheat crackers with turkey and veggie chili for lunch*
- *Food: Edamame*
- *Roasted bell peppers, onions, and zucchini with baked chicken for dinner*

Day 4:
- Sweet potato hash with eggs for breakfast
- Snack: Cottage cheese with slices of pineapple.

- Grilled shrimp skewers for lunch with quinoa salad (feta cheese, cherry tomatoes, and cucumber)
- Snack: Trail mix with dried fruit and almonds.
- Stir-fried vegetables and tofu with brown rice for dinner.

Day 5:
- Whole grain bread and an egg and vegetable scramble for breakfast
- Snack: Salt-and-pepper roasted almonds
- Baked fish with a gratin of broccoli and cauliflower for lunch.
- Snack: Bites of banana and almond butter
- Sweet potato-topped lentil and vegetable shepherd's pie for dinner

Day 6:
- A Greek yogurt parfait for breakfast with fruit and granola.
- Snack: Guacamole and sliced bell pepper.
- Grilled portobello mushroom and vegetable wrap for lunch
- Snack: Nutritional yeast-topped popcorn
- Acorn squash packed with quinoa, cranberries, and walnuts for dinner

Day 7:
- Overnight oats with almond butter and banana for breakfast
- Snack: Feta cheese and cherry tomatoes.
- Whole wheat tortilla wraps with turkey and avocado for lunch.
- Snack: Nut- and dried fruit-filled energy balls

- Grilled chicken and roasted veggies (broccoli, bell peppers, and carrots) for dinner

THIRD WEEK

Day 1:
- Greek yogurt with mixed berries and chia seeds for breakfast.
- Snack: Hummus-topped carrot sticks.
- Grilled chicken salad with vegetables and mixed greens for lunch.
- Apple slices with almond butter, number five.
- Baked fish and roasted veggies for dinner

Day 2:
- Whole grain toast and an omelet with vegetables for breakfast.
- Snack: Salt-and-pepper roasted almonds
- For lunch, have a chickpea salad with tomatoes and cucumbers.
- Snack: Cucumber slices and tzatziki sauce.
- Brown rice and grilled tofu kebabs for dinner.

Day 3:
- Overnight oats with almond milk, fruit, and almonds for breakfast. Turkey and cheese roll-ups for a snack.
- Whole-grain bread and lentil and vegetable soup for lunch
- Food: Edamame
- Quinoa and spinach salad for dinner with grilled salmon

Day 4:

- Whole grain oats with sliced banana and almonds for breakfast
- Greek yogurt with honey and granola for a snack.
- Grilled shrimp skewers for lunch, along with an avocado and tomato salad
- Snack: Nutritional yeast-topped popcorn
- Stir-fried vegetables and tofu with brown rice for dinner.

Day 5:
- A frittata with vegetables and feta cheese for breakfast
- Roasted chickpeas as a snack.
- Whole wheat tortilla wraps with turkey and avocado for lunch.
- Snack: A fruit salad with honey and Greek yogurt.
- Roasted veggies and chicken on the grill for dinner

Day 6:
- A parfait of berries and Greek yogurt with granola for breakfast
- Snack: Homemade trail mix with dried fruit and nuts
- Baked sweet potato with berries and Greek yogurt for lunch.
- Snack: Hummus-topped carrot sticks.
- Whole wheat tortillas and lentil and veggie tacos for supper.

Day 7:
- Whole grain waffles with fresh berries and Greek yogurt for breakfast.
- Snack: Nut- and dried fruit-filled energy balls
- Goat cheese and grilled vegetable quesadillas for lunch.
- Snack: Guacamole and sliced bell pepper

- Dinner will be baked salmon over a gratin of broccoli and cauliflower.

FOURTH WEEK

Day 1
- Greek yogurt with mixed berries and nuts for breakfast
- Grilled chicken salad for lunch with various greens and veggies and a vinaigrette dressing.
- Snack: Hummus-topped carrot sticks.
- Roasted veggies and salmon on a grill for dinner.

Day 2
- Baked egg and veggie bowls for breakfast
- For lunch, a turkey and avocado wrap with a side salad and a whole wheat tortilla.
- Snack: Granola and honey-topped Greek yogurt
- Brown rice and vegetable stir-fry for dinner.

Day 3
- Protein-rich chocolate-banana pancakes for breakfast
- Lunch: Carrot and celery in lentil soup
- Food: Edamame
- Grilled shrimp skewers with quinoa salad for dinner.

Day 4
- Avocado toast with tomatoes and sprouts for breakfast
- Baked sweet potato with berries and Greek yogurt for lunch.
- Snack: Salt-and-pepper roasted almonds
- Tuna salad on whole-wheat bread with mixed greens for dinner.

Day 5

- For breakfast, have a spinach and feta omelet. 2. For lunch, have brown rice and chickpea curry.
- Snack of almond butter-dipped apple slices
- Brown rice and grilled tofu kebabs for dinner.

Day 6

- Blueberry protein waffles for breakfast
- Brown rice and mixed veggie stir-fry for lunch.
- Snack: Squares of dark chocolate
- Grilled chicken and veggie kabobs for dinner

Day 7

- Overnight oats with almond butter and banana for breakfast
- Fish and boiled veggies for lunch.
- Greek yogurt with mixed berries and nuts as a snack.
- A shepherd's pie with sweet potato on top and lentils for dinner

Note: This meal plan is only a recommendation; you should make changes under your needs and preferences. To choose the appropriate meal plan for controlling excessive triglycerides, speaking with a registered dietitian or other healthcare professional is critical.

CONCLUSION

A diet high in triglycerides can help lower blood triglyceride levels, which reduces the risk of heart disease and other health issues. Limiting the consumption of saturated and trans fats, boosting the consumption of fiber and omega-3 fatty acids, and lowering the consumption of sugar and processed carbohydrates are essential components of a high triglycerides diet.

Lean proteins, whole grains, fruits, vegetables, lean meats, and healthy fats can all be included in a diet to help lower triglyceride levels while supplying the body with the necessary nutrients. Limiting the consumption of alcohol and processed, high-fat foods is also crucial because these foods can raise triglyceride levels.

Planning meals and snacks might help you follow a diet high in triglycerides. Preparing delectable, gratifying, and heart-healthy meals is feasible with imagination and experimentation. A licensed dietitian or healthcare professional can offer individualized advice and help control triglyceride levels through dietary adjustments.

Made in the USA
Columbia, SC
10 April 2024